Every Day with Jesus

NOV/DEC 2017

The God of All Comfort

'comforts us in all our troubles, so that we can comfort those in any trouble'
2 Corinthians 1:3–4

Selwyn Hughes
Revised and updated by Mick Brooks

CWR, Waverley Abbey House, Waverley Lane, Farnham, Surrey GU9 8EP, UK **Tel: 01252 784700**
Email: mail@cwr.org.uk Registered Charity No. 294387. Registered Limited Company No. 1990308.

Cover image: istockphoto.com
Quiet Time image: istockphoto.com
Printed in England by Linney

Every Day with Jesus is available in large print from CWR. It is also available on **audio and DAISY** in the UK and Eire for the sole use of those with a visual impairment worse than N12, or who are registered blind. For details please contact **Torch Trust for the Blind**, Tel: 01858 438260. Torch House, Torch Way, Northampton Road, Market Harborough LE16 9HL.

A word of introduction...

In recent years I have found myself in conversation with wide-eyed, fresh-faced health professionals, whose opening question invariably is, 'Do you have any allergies?' My most usual response is, 'Yes, I'm allergic to pain.' This is normally met with a mildly quizzical response!

I have learnt, however, that pain can be a gift from God. It's our inbuilt warning system that tells us something could be wrong, either physically or emotionally, and that something needs attention. I have also discovered, thankfully, that God is the God of all comfort.

His comfort is much more than the comfort blanket or favourite soft toy that a small child clings to. It's a presence that brings strong reassurance and builds confidence. God's comfort brings hope.

This issue, written from Selwyn's own personal experience, helps us explore some of the many struggles and difficulties of life that may result in us experiencing pain. Selwyn – who outlived his wife and their two sons, and himself suffered with terminal cancer – was no stranger to emotional and physical pain. He understood that God's divine presence, when invited, can make all the difference when handling the painful situations that come into our lives.

In these closing months of the year, it's my prayer that as you read these devotions, you too will discover that our Father is the God of all comfort.

Mick

Mick Brooks, Consulting Editor

Free small group resource to accompany this issue can be found at www.cwr.org.uk/extra

The *EDWJ* Facebook community is growing!
To join the conversation visit www.facebook.com/edwjpage

The choice is always ours

WED
1 NOV

FOR READING & MEDITATION – 2 CORINTHIANS 7:1–16

'Godly sorrow brings repentance that leads to salvation... but worldly sorrow brings death.' (v10)

In this last issue of another year, we look at the way in which God is able to take pain caused by deep hurts, sadness or distress that may occur in our lives and use it to bring about a good and godly resolution. We all need to understand this because sooner or later everyone has to deal with pain in one form or another.

From today's passage we learn that the ungodly behaviour of the Corinthian community had caused great pain to the apostle Paul, and so with deep sorrow he had written to them about their need to change. His words, in turn, brought great pain to their hearts, but under God it led them to repentance. Paul then explains that when we turn to God in our pain He can bring about His resolutions. Those who try to deal with the pain they are feeling on an entirely human level will find it ultimately brings no true rest to the soul. Those who take their pain to God will discover the God of all comfort. *The Message* translates today's text in this way: 'Distress that drives us to God does that. It turns us around. It gets us back in the way of salvation. We never regret that kind of pain. But those who let distress drive them away from God are full of regrets, end up on a deathbed of regrets.' When we open ourselves up to God and bring our pain to Him, it gives Him the opportunity to turn what would have been senseless suffering into a spiritual discipline.

When we experience pain, the question is not so much 'where has it come from?' but 'where is it going?'. And where it goes is determined by whether we allow it to turn us to more pain or God. The choice is always ours.

FURTHER STUDY

Deut. 30:11–20; Phil. 1:12–18

1. What choices does Moses set before God's people?

2. How is Paul able to rejoice, even while in prison?

Lord Jesus, help me to put every pain or distress that comes into my life in Your hands. I pray that You, who turned Your cross into a throne, would help me turn my suffering into strength also. For Your own dear name's sake. Amen.

THURS
2 NOV

Hidden pain

FOR READING & MEDITATION – PSALM 69:29–36

'I am in pain and distress; may your salvation, O God, protect me.' (v29)

Yesterday we ended by saying that the question is not so much 'where has my pain come from?' as 'where is it going?'. This is never to make light of pain or to dodge the issue of why a loving and omnipotent God created a universe in which pain now exists. To go into the reasons why God allowed pain to become part of life on earth is beyond the scope of these devotional readings; my concern here is to help you take God into your pain and allow Him to turn whatever pain you might be experiencing (or will experience in the future) to good ends. My focus will be on the mental and emotional pains that arise within us, though I will have something to add concerning physical pain also.

Some of the worst pains a human being has to bear are emotional pains – the anxiety that burns like fire, the loneliness that engulfs us like a black cloud, the dull ache that affects our whole outlook. Day by day, men and women are leading their lives as normal (and often doing so with a brave smile), while all the time their calm exterior is hiding a lacerated heart. Everyone knows that it is far easier to say 'My tooth is aching' than 'My heart is broken'. Sadly, in the absence of anything to see, people do not often offer support or special care.

Not many of us can respond to pain with praise and thanksgiving as we find the psalmist doing in today's text. His godly reaction may not be ours, but perhaps in the days that lie ahead we will learn some things that will help us respond in the same way.

FURTHER STUDY

Psa. 34:1–10; 1 Pet. 4:12–19

1. Why does David boast in the Lord?

2. How can Christians rise above all suffering, according to Peter?

My Father and my God, help me to learn from the psalmist and rise above all my pains – mental, emotional and even physical – and turn them into praise. In Jesus' name. Amen.

Life is unjust

FOR READING & MEDITATION – JOHN 16:17–33

'In this world you will have trouble. But take heart! I have overcome the world.' (v33)

As we have been saying, although our pain may have roots outside of ourselves, we need not necessarily focus too much on where it has come from but where it is leading us. Sadly, some people are never able to get past their distress because they say to themselves: 'This is unjust. I did nothing to bring this on myself, so why do I have to bear it?' Certainly, for many people the pain is unjust, but sadly we cannot expect life to be always fair. Jesus doesn't teach that it is. On the contrary, at its heart there is a cross – and that is the world's supreme injustice. Because we live in a fallen world, our prayers should be for justice, strength, creativity and interventions to turn injustice to good ends. Then we will experience something greater than justice – we will experience the blessing of God.

Life certainly didn't seem 'just' for the apostle Paul. He found it brought him all kinds of difficulties – imprisonments, floggings, desertions, anxiety, and so on. It wasn't just. But he found something better than justice. 'In all things God works for the good of those who love him,' he told us in his letter to the Romans (8:28). The things that happened to him were not good; some of them were hurled at him by the devil himself. But God worked all these things into a pattern for good that brought glory to Him and aided Paul's spiritual growth. 'Like two cogs working together,' says one preacher, 'God actually uses evil for the destruction of evil. He uses devil-sourced evil for the making of God-inspired men and women.' Let's learn with God's help to turn every pain into a pearl and set out on this journey of discovery and growth.

FURTHER STUDY

Gen. 45:3–13; 50:20; 1 Pet. 2:18–25

1. How did all things work together for good for Joseph?

2. How did Jesus face unjust suffering?

Lord Jesus Christ, You came into an unjust and fallen world and showed us how to turn every obstacle into an opportunity. Please help me learn to ask not just for justice but by Your grace to follow Your example. Amen.

SAT
4 NOV

Pain – an ally

FOR READING & MEDITATION – PSALM 71:1–24

'Though you have made me see troubles, many and bitter, you will restore my life again' (v20)

Although, as we have said, our purpose in these meditations is not to explore in depth why pain was introduced into the universe, there can be little doubt, in my opinion, that were it not for physical pain the human race would have become extinct long ago. If disease did not cause us pain, we would think nothing about it and would let it run its course until it was too late to do anything about it. It has a purpose, even though it hurts. Physical pain, unpleasant though it may be, turns out to be our friendly watchman guarding us against life's many dangers. Someone has described pain as 'God's preventative grace built into the structure of our physical life to warn us of danger ahead.'

That may apply to physical pain, but what about emotional pain and distress – can that be a danger signal too? In many cases, I think it is. The pain that comes from certain forms of emotional distress may be a warning sign indicating that life is not being lived in the way God intended. I once spoke to a man who told me the best thing that had happened to him was to fall into depression. The type of depression he suffered from was not clinical depression that comes from a chemical imbalance, but the type that develops from holding a jaundiced view of oneself and the world around. 'My depression,' he told me, 'was a signal that I needed to reshape my lifestyle and change my way of thinking. When I did so, the depression fell away – mission accomplished.' This man's depression brought about challenge and change. In his life it became a blessing in disguise.

Pain need not always be regarded as an enemy – it may become our ally in gaining a better and fuller life.

FURTHER STUDY

Psa. 116:1–9; Rom. 8:35–39

1. How does the psalmist react to trouble and sorrow?

2. Of what is Paul convinced?

Gracious Father, help me understand that in Your universe You allow only what You can use. Even in pain and suffering You have an authentic word to speak to me. Please help me hear it. In Jesus' name. Amen.

CWR Ministry Events

PLEASE PRAY FOR THE TEAM

DATE	EVENT	PLACE	PRESENTER(S)
2 Nov	Reaching the Next Generation	Waverley Abbey House	Andy Peck and Martin Saunders
11 Nov	People Coming Alongside People	WAH	Trevor J. Partridge
13–17 Nov	Introduction to Biblical Care and Counselling	WAH	John Munt and Rosalyn Derges
16 Nov	Nurturing the Church for Growth	WAH	Andy Peck
18 Nov	Understanding Yourself, Understanding Others	WAH	Rosalyn Derges and Lynette Brooks
22 Nov	Great Chapters of the Bible	WAH	Philip Greenslade
23 Nov	The Bible in a Day	WAH	Andy Peck
24–26 Nov	Inspiring Women Advent Weekend: The Promise, the Expectation and the Wonder	WAH	Inspiring Women team
30 Nov	Pastoring on the Fringe	WAH	Andy Peck
5 Dec	Inspiring Women Christmas Celebration	Pilgrim Hall	Fiona Castle and the Inspiring Women team
7 Dec	Inspiring Women Christmas Celebration	WAH	Fiona Castle and the Inspiring Women team
8 Dec	Hearing God's Voice	WAH	Andy Peck
23–27 Dec	Christmas at Pilgrim Hall	PH	Pilgrim Hall team

Please pray for our students and tutors on our ongoing BA Counselling programme at Waverley Abbey College (which takes place at Waverley Abbey House and Pilgrim Hall), as well as our Certificate in Christian Counselling and MA Counselling qualifications.

We would also appreciate prayer for our ongoing ministry in Singapore and Cambodia, as well as the many regional events that will be happening around the UK this year.

For further information and a full list of CWR's courses, seminars and events, call **+44 (0)1252 784719** or visit **www.cwr.org.uk/courses**

You can also download our free Prayer Track, which includes daily prayers, from **www.cwr.org.uk/prayertrack**

SUN
5 NOV

Attitude is everything

FOR READING & MEDITATION – PSALM 34:1–22

'The LORD is close to the broken-hearted and saves those who are crushed in spirit.' (v18)

Pain and suffering, both physical and emotional, is, we are saying, experienced by us all – good and bad alike. But while the same type of experiences come to us all, they do not have the same effect upon us all. The same thing can happen to two different people but the effect on them may be quite different. It all depends on their attitudes. As someone has commented, 'What life does to us in the long run depends upon what life finds in us.'

In a church where I was once the pastor, there were two men, both Christians, who were partners in a firm that, through no fault of theirs went bankrupt. One became sad and withdrawn and had to have significant help and support for a whole year in order to overcome his emotional difficulties. The other, though sad, reasoned that even though the bankruptcy was not their fault, he could still learn valuable lessons from it that would help him be more careful in the future. He went out to look for another job, made a success of it, and in time was able to use some of the money he earned to pay off all his creditors. The same event but with opposite outcomes.

So often in life it is not the actions of others that break us but our reactions to the actions of others. Let's not forget that. Emotional distress can make some people bitter, whereas others it sweetens and refines. It's our response that's important, and whether or not we are willing to let God enter our pain and turn it to good ends. One thing we can be sure of: God stands by to comfort us in our pain and He is waiting to help us extract the gold from the ore of painful experiences and bear fruit to His glory (John 15:8).

FURTHER STUDY

Rom. 12:1–3; Eph. 4:20–28

1. Of what transformation does Paul speak?

2. Where does a new attitude of mind come from?

Lord God, forgive me if I try to handle the pain of life in my own strength when You are waiting to help me transform my pain and guide it towards positive ends. Amen.

Light on a dark problem

FOR READING & MEDITATION – JOHN 8:12–20

'I am the light of the world. Whoever follows me will never walk in darkness, but will have the light of life.' (v12)

The major truth we hold on to in these meditations on 'The God of all comfort', is the importance of turning our pain over into His hands. In our hands pain is a problem; in His hands it is a possibility. On 1 November, we saw from our reading that when we look to God to guide us through the pain it can lead to life, but when we do not allow Him to direct us it can lead to darkness. Every happening can take us in one of two directions – towards death or life. As someone has put it, 'The commonplaces of life make us either common – or Christian.'

A successful businessman with a large house and a big bank balance was asked by his wife to look out of the window at the beautiful sunset. For a few seconds he looked at the red streaks in the sky and then remarked, 'Yes, lovely... it reminds me to ask you to tell the cook that my bacon should be more streaky.' He turned a radiant sunset into a reminder of bacon! We can either make the glorious commonplace or the commonplace glorious – depending on whether or not we are willing to bring God into all that happens in our lives, especially our pains. In the case of the couple mentioned above, the woman looked upwards and saw God's artistry, the man looked inwards and thought only of his appetite.

FURTHER STUDY

Psa. 4:1–8; Eph. 5:8–15

1. How does the psalmist pray when in distress?

2. In what ways does Christ's light shine on us?

In today's text Jesus declared that He is the light of the world. He was and is! The more I have listened to theories concerning pain, the more I have come to realise that Jesus is the one who throws light on this, the darkest of problems. To be able to use pain – this is transformative. The one who gave us this power is indeed the light of the world.

Lord Jesus, You who spoke the word of light when life seemed dark and mysterious, please help me to live in that light, especially when my soul or body are racked with pain. Amen.

Christians not exempt

FOR READING & MEDITATION – PSALM 51:1–19

'Surely you desire truth in the inner parts; you teach me wisdom in the inmost place.' (v6)

As a first-hand observer of Christian life over a period of six decades, I have been intrigued by the different ways in which people go about dealing with the mental and emotional pains that they wrestle with. Some, for example, live in denial, trying to suppress or repress the fact that they are experiencing any pain – whether emotional, spiritual or physical – just as David in today's psalm had tried to bury his pain. Sadly, when we repress or suppress or even deny the pain, it frequently results in further problems.

Some say that a real Christian, who walks in an intimate relationship with God day by day and has a rich prayer life, need never feel any emotional pain. This is, I believe, is simply not true. Admittedly, Christians who are walking with God are much more able to resolve the kind of pain that those who do not know God feel when making wrong moral choices, but their relationship with God does not prevent them experiencing the pain that comes from such things as rejection, bereavement, misunderstanding, and so on. Nor does it exempt them from the pain that comes from the very fact that as Christians they stand out as being different from the world and have a moral compass that others perhaps laugh at because of their faith.

FURTHER STUDY

Mark 3:1–6; 7:31–35; 8:11–12; 2 Cor. 1:3–11

1. What painful realities did Jesus face?
2. From what painful realities was Paul not exempt?

When explaining to Christians that it is quite normal to feel pain when ridiculed or insulted, they respond by saying that Scripture teaches we are to rejoice when persecuted. That may be so, but we do not need to pretend we feel no pain in order to rejoice. Such people live in denial and fail to realise that integrity requires that whatever is true must be faced.

Father God, help me not to deny the existence of anything unpleasant or painful in my life but to rise above it through Your strength and grace. Make me a person of complete integrity, dear Lord. In Jesus' name. Amen.

Mender of broken hearts

FOR READING & MEDITATION – PSALM 119:49–56

'My comfort in my suffering is this: Your promise preserves my life.' (v50)

Yesterday we noted that some people may use denial to deal with their pain. But any course of action other than turning to God will end in frustration.

Some turn to literature when their hearts are aching. While I was a pastor in central London, I was told about an elderly woman whose husband had just died, and so I made a visit to her home. I found her surrounded by a pile of books that someone had given her to help her deal with the pain of her loss. 'You'll find comfort in these books,' promised the well-wisher who had given them to her. No doubt this person was a lover of literature herself and had found rich enjoyment from books, but the widowed woman told me she had read for hours without finding a single word of comfort. I can still recall how sad I felt as I saw the expression on her face – an expression of deep disappointment and dejection.

I count myself a book-lover and regard books as some of my dearest possessions. There are hundreds of well-thumbed volumes on my shelves. It's wonderful to rub shoulders with writers of past generations – C.S. Lewis, Winston Churchill, Charles Finney, William Shakespeare, and my favourite writers of all – the Welsh revivalists. Yet I have to admit that for all my love of literature and my indebtedness to the great writers of the past, in the hours when my wife, my father, and my two sons were taken from this world, literature could not and did not provide adequate comfort. John Henry Newman, the master stylist and superb writer, once said, 'Literature may be a good supplement but it cannot mend a broken heart.' How true.

FURTHER STUDY

Psa. 147:1–11; Eccles. 12:9–14; John 14:16–21, 25–27

1. How does the psalmist draw on God's never-failing resources?

2. How does Jesus prepare the disciples for their impending loss?

Lord Jesus, healer of pain and mender of broken hearts, I am so glad that I can draw from Your never-failing resources when my heart is filled with pain. All honour and glory be to Your wonderful name. Amen.

THURS
9 NOV

Soothing is not healing

FOR READING & MEDITATION – ISAIAH 51:1–8

'The LORD will surely comfort Zion and will look with compassion on all her ruins' (v3)

We continue considering the sources of comfort people choose to go to, other than God, in an attempt to deal with their pain. Some, when their hearts are hurting, turn to nature. They believe the comfort they need can be found in gazing upon majestic scenery or studying the universe. Many have told me that in times of great pain they have found solace in walking through the countryside, and who will deny that the beauty of nature can minister to us? The solace that nature provides, however, is only temporary. I myself have felt greatly uplifted when walking in the countryside, but nature is no cure for a broken heart.

Those fascinated by science claim that a study of the universe with all its intricate and marvellous complexities can fill the mind with so much awe that pain can be squeezed out. A sentence from a book written many years ago by Lord Avebury entitled *The Marvels of the Universe* has stayed with me over the years, and as far as I can remember it went something like this: 'The universe will do much to soothe, comfort and console the troubles and sorrows of life.' I learned from that book all about the polycystins and the foraminifera and I extended my knowledge of the dinosaur and the diplodocus, but I never regarded it as something that could deal effectively with any pain.

If the study of the marvels of the universe is a comfort then it is a cold comfort. Though it may distract a heart in pain it cannot heal it. 'The stars,' as my old mentor Dr W.E. Sangster used to point out, 'can neither love nor laugh, nor weep. They only shine, and they shine with indifference on our joy and woe.'

FURTHER STUDY

Gen. 9:8–17; Job 31:26–28; Psa. 29:1–11; Jonah 2:1–9

1. In what ways does David celebrate the Lord?
2. Study Jonah's prayer as he turns in distress to the Lord.

Gracious and loving God, how thankful I am that in my pain I can turn not just to creation but to the one who created it, and find in You the strength and healing I need for my soul. My heart is Yours forever. Amen.

Numbing the pain

FOR READING & MEDITATION – 2 THESSALONIANS 2:13–17

'May our Lord Jesus Christ... encourage your hearts and strengthen you' (vv16–17)

Some people, when they find their hearts filled with pain, turn to drink. Behind this, in part, is a desire to forget. For others, they may turn to spending sprees, overindulging in food, or attention-seeking behaviour, in effort to suppress any hurt or gain a kind of comfort. But these things, in reality, only aggravate the trouble they are intended to heal. There is only one place where we can receive true comfort, hope and restoration, and that is in the arms of Jesus.

Once, when I was ministering at a church weekend retreat, I remember being deeply impressed with the woman who led the worship over the three days I was there. She appeared to me to be mature, competent, and very spiritual. On the last day, she asked if she could speak to me privately, and I was somewhat taken aback when, during our conversation, she said she was an alcoholic. 'How did your alcoholism start?' I asked. She told me that she had once had an abortion and was haunted by continual guilt and shame over that decision. As a means for numbing her pain, she had used alcohol on a daily basis ever since.

As we talked together it was clear that she already knew that the drink could no more deal with her pain than an aspirin can cure cancer, and I was able to assure her that God is willing to forgive – something she knew in theory but somehow had never accepted. With relief and thankfulness she received the forgiveness God offers and found complete freedom from her alcoholism and the shame that had riddled her soul.

FURTHER STUDY

Psa. 32:1–11; Isa. 12:1–6

1. How should the godly pray, according to the psalmist?

2. How can God's people express their joy?

Loving Lord, how can I ever thank You enough that You not only forgive us when we confess to You our sin but You restore to us the joy of our salvation? Your goodness and love are my constant hope. Amen.

SAT
11 NOV

Art has no arms

FOR READING & MEDITATION – DEUTERONOMY 33:24–29

'The eternal God is your refuge, and underneath are the everlasting arms.' (v27)

Today we continue looking at some of the different places people go and the things they do in order to relieve their personal pain. Some people when in pain turn to art. They seek a remedy in art galleries, in theatres, in listening to music or gazing at sculptures, but as with literature and beautiful scenery, these things are merely supplements and can never be substitutes. They provide a degree of comfort but they can never heal in the true sense of the word.

Whenever one particular lady I used to know experienced pain, as a result of some problem that had arisen in her life or relationships, she would listen over and over again to the *Hallelujah Chorus* from Handel's oratorio *The Messiah*. But when talking with her, I found that it was the music she looked to for healing of her pain rather than the reminder that 'the Lord God omnipotent reigneth', who alone could deal effectively with her pain.

While researching this subject of the ways in which people attempt to deal with their pain, I read of Heinrich Heine, the German poet who loved all things beautiful. When going through a personal crisis in which his heart was filled with pain, he knelt before the famous statue known as the Venus de Milo and held out his hands to that serene torso. But after a while he confessed in tears, 'It is beautiful, but it has no arms.' Art has no arms to lift us up in the hour when pain cuts deep into the soul. The most beautiful sculpture, the most exquisite painting, the most wonderful music – each of these things is powerless to reach into a soul that has been engulfed in pain and bring permanent healing and relief.

FURTHER STUDY

Exod. 2:23–25; 3:7–14; Deut. 4:32–40; James 4:7–10

1. What kind of God revealed Himself to Moses?
2. Of what kind of God does Moses speak?

Eternal Father, strong to save, accept my gratitude once again for the truth that when I am in pain and my arms stretch out to You, I find that Your arms are always outstretched to me. Amen.

'Poor me'

FOR READING & MEDITATION – PSALM 69:1–20

'Scorn has broken my heart and has left me helpless; I looked for sympathy, but there was none' (v20)

Another road down which people may travel in order to deal with their pain is that of self-pity. One psychologist described this as 'easily the most destructive of the non-pharmaceutical narcotics'. Self-pity protects us from pain by allowing us to comfort ourselves with statements such as, 'I'm a victim', 'No one loves me', 'I'm always the one getting hurt', and so on, which in turn leads to 'poor me'. Self-pity acts as an anaesthetic for our pain by momentarily separating us from reality and enabling us to see ourselves as a victim rather than an agent.

The difference between being a victim and an agent is not always understood, but often in life (not always) we play the part of the victim, when in reality we have been the agent who has, in some measure at least, brought about our difficulties. I once counselled a woman who felt, 'Everyone is against me, it seems, and almost all the people I talk to object to what I am saying and take the opposite view of things.' The truth of the matter was that she was against everyone else. She was critical, abusive, sarcastic, insensitive, cynical and obstructive, and was difficult with everyone she came into contact with.

FURTHER STUDY

1 Kings 19:3–12; Acts 26:9–18

1. What is God's answer to Elijah's self-pity?

2. How real is Paul in his defence before Agrippa?

As you can imagine, this woman did not have much success in her relationships. When people avoided her and sometimes rejected her, she lapsed into self-pity and consoled herself by saying, 'Poor me... I have to carry this cross all the time because people just don't care about me as they should.' The cross was, in part, one of her own making. She saw herself as a victim but in reality she was an agent. Self-pity may soothe and protect but it cannot heal.

Dear God, save me I pray from self-pity whenever my heart is in pain. And help me to discern whether the pain I experience when I feel I am a victim is really due to the fact that I may have been an agent. Please help me be real. Amen.

You can be a HOPE giver

For many years, CWR has sent resources into prisons to help those seeking answers and direction, and introduce them to the God who loves them.

'For God did not send his Son into the world to condemn the world, but to save the world through him.' John 3:17

We are continually amazed by the correspondence we receive from prisoners, describing how they have been deeply impacted by learning more about God and His Word through our resources. They are discovering an eternal hope behind prison doors, and it is our desire to see many more experience the same.

Will you join us as we partner with Prison Hope, an initiative working to connect the Church with local prisons? Together we have published *40 Stories of Hope*, a book of testimonies from prisoners and their family members, which encourage and inspire faith. Stories like this...

'In a somewhat dazed state, the clunk of the cell door behind me brought me to my senses and I realised that life as I had known it had changed forever... Then I later received a book as a gift.

Within it was a verse of Scripture that changed everything for me – Jeremiah 29:11: "'For I know the plans I have for you,' declares the Lord, *'plans to prosper you and not to harm you, plans to give you hope and a future.'" From the moment I read it, I realised that God was with me, and He listens to, and answers, my prayers. Since then He has taken me on an amazing spiritual journey to a place of peace, joy and contentment that I could never have imagined.'*

We want to make transformation like this possible for thousands of other prisoners today.

Send hope into prisons

For just £40 a box, you can send 20 copies of *40 Stories of Hope* to those in prison. Why not get involved as a group or church? Find out more at **www.cwr.org/donate**

Also available as individual copies, *40 Stories of Hope* is ideal for Lent as the 40 entries can be read daily in the run up to Easter. Be inspired yourself, or give a book away to encourage a friend or neighbour.

ISBN: 978-1-78259-759-9

RRP: £7.99

Available to buy from Christian bookshops or direct from CWR at **www.cwr.org.uk/store**

God's design reversed

FOR READING & MEDITATION – 1 THESSALONIANS 4:1–12

'It is God's will that you should be sanctified: that you should avoid sexual immorality' (v3)

Another way in which people deal with pain is through inappropriate sexual experiences. It is not without some hesitation that I focus on this subject, but it is clear that some people do struggle with this. We live in a world, society and culture that over time has almost completely reversed God's original design for relationships. Let me try and briefly explain.

God originally created us to relate to one another in oneness at the level of our spirit, our soul and then our bodies. Drawing first from God all the love and strength that He supplies, from a place of fullness we can then reach out spirit to spirit with God's *agape* love to one another. This kind of relationship is energised by God's selfless unconditional love, enabling us to then build a relationship at the level of our soul, thoughts, feelings and decisions. And then, finally, in the context of a lifelong commitment in marriage, we can experience oneness in our physical relationships. However, the world has completely reversed the order to body, soul then maybe spirit. This creates innumerable complications and, in many cases, considerable pain and distress in people's relationships.

Sex is God's gift, and practised within His boundaries it can lift the feelings to great heights of pleasure and satisfaction. Some, however, use sexual promiscuity as a painkiller and try to deal with their emotional discomfort by focusing on sexual desires in a way that is not intended by God. When faced with these kinds of temptations, let's call upon the resources of God's grace and help.

FURTHER STUDY

Job 31:1–12; Matt. 5:27–30; 1 Cor. 6:12–20

1. How seriously does Jesus regard illicit sexual stimulation?
2. What reasons does Paul give for fleeing from sexual immorality?

Lord God, help me not to allow sexual thoughts to distract me or drown out Your still, small voice. I offer myself to You again. Please give me wisdom and power to do what is right. In Jesus' name. Amen.

Misusing desire

FOR READING & MEDITATION – LUKE 15:11–32

'his father... was filled with compassion for him; he ran to his son, threw his arms around him and kissed him.' (v20)

For one more day we are going to consider the consequences of reversing God's order for relationships and using our sexual desires wrongly as a way of numbing our pain. Most psychologists recognise that our physical appetites – food, drink and sex – when over-indulged are very effective at temporarily numbing pain. This is one of the reasons why pornography is increasingly a major problem, not just in the wider society but also within the Christian community.

When speaking at a men's meeting once I asked the men present to close their eyes and raise their hands if they were struggling with pornography. Almost a quarter of those attending the meeting raised their hands. Their honesty impressed me, but also saddened me. After the meeting I talked to one man who sought me out for advice. He admitted, 'Whenever I am in pain I turn to pornographic material... and for a time all the pain goes away.' It has a similar effect to excessive alcohol – albeit unconsciously, it temporarily relieves the soul of pain. However, it's only temporary. The pain returns and the scene is set for repetitive and addictive behaviours to develop. This is further compounded and complicated by the surrounding circumstances of this destructive and dangerous 'painkiller'.

I urge those of you who do not seek this form of pain relief to be aware of becoming judgmental; rather, join me today in praying for those who do struggle to ease their pain by the misuse of sexual desires. But if this is you today, bring it to the Father now. Give Him your pain and your struggles and allow Him to hold you and walk with you. Then will you find freedom and rest.

FURTHER STUDY

Matt. 4:1–11; Rom. 10:6–13

1. How did Jesus find wisdom and courage when tempted?

2. What happens to those who call on the name of the Lord?

Heavenly Father, help me now to relate and live in the way that You've designed me to do, to give all my pain to You and allow You to hold me in my pain. Then, with Your help I can find new solutions and resolutions. In Jesus' name. Amen.

WED
15 NOV

'Wave to me, William'

FOR READING & MEDITATION – PSALM 25:16–22

'Turn to me and be gracious to me, for I am lonely and afflicted.' (v16)

Having looked at some of the supposed sources of comfort to which people turn in order to deal with their inner pain, we move on now to consider some of the most serious pains that can arise in people's lives. The first I refer to is the pain of loneliness. It is both a desolate and bleak place to be. Those who have experienced loneliness know how acute the pain is. Mother Teresa said on one occasion that the world's greatest disease is not Aids or cancer or any similar thing – it is loneliness.

I have often used the story of the poet Rupert Brooke, who was about to set sail from Liverpool to New York. He felt very lonely because no one had come to see him off, yet all around him people were saying goodbye to their friends. Looking around, he noticed a small homeless child and discovered his name was William. 'William,' he said, 'will you wave to me if I give you sixpence?' 'Yes,' said the little boy. After the sixpence had changed hands and the poet had boarded the ship, the little boy took out a dirty rag from his pocket and began to wave. As the ship moved away from the landing stage, Rupert Brooke said he got his six-pennyworth as he saw little William's dirty rag waving amidst the white handkerchiefs of the others bidding their friends farewell.

Some people may regard that story as somewhat extreme, but they are likely to be the people who have never felt lonely. So many people who have been born into a large family or have the gift of making friends easily do not know what it means to long for community and companionship. Pray for lonely people today and look for opportunities to reach out to them.

FURTHER STUDY

Psa. 27:7–14; John 16:25–32

1. Of what is the psalmist confident?

2. In whom is Jesus confident?

Gracious Lord, I pray today for all those who find themselves bereft of friends and are experiencing the pain of loneliness. Strong Son of God, draw close to them I pray. Amen.

Jesus knows

FOR READING & MEDITATION – HEBREWS 4:12–16

'For we do not have a high priest who is unable to sympathise with our weaknesses' (v15)

The awful thing about loneliness is that it is possible to be in the midst of many people (in an active church, for instance) and still feel lonely. Strangely, the feeling of loneliness can be intensified in a crowd. One woman told me: 'The moment when the Sunday morning service is over is the worst moment for me. Everyone seems to make for their friends and there is the hubbub of happy conversations going on, but often I have no one to speak to and this makes me feel doubly lonely.' Isn't it sad that in church – the one place where you would think love and friendship would flow to all and through all – a person can still feel lonely.

Of course, we have to admit that some people are lonely because they may not have the skills needed to develop friendships. However, I am talking now about those who, even though they are friendly individuals, find themselves for different reasons cut off from agreeable companionship.

Is Jesus able to enter into the pain of those who feel almost permanently lonely? With all my heart I believe that He is. Some theologians claim that Jesus knew loneliness as no one before or since. I share that view. Imagine, they say, how He must have felt after leaving the throne of God and living amongst sinful men and women. It is not possible for us to conceive all the feelings that Jesus' descent from heaven to earth would have provoked in Him, but it is easy to imagine (for me at least) that He knew more than anyone else the feelings of loneliness, and in His humanity He valued the friendship of His disciples. The Son of God knows how to comfort the lonely, for He has trodden the way of loneliness Himself.

FURTHER STUDY

Psa. 146:1–10; Mark 14:27–38

1. To whom does the Lord give help?

2. In what circumstances did Jesus find Himself alone?

Lord Jesus, thank You for understanding and sharing in the pain of loneliness. Help me to reach out to you first when I am facing this kind of pain, and to be a friend of others who are longing for companionship. Amen.

FRI
17 NOV

The perfect sympathiser

FOR READING & MEDITATION – HEBREWS 2:10–18

'Because he himself suffered when he was tempted, he is able to help those who are being tempted.' (v18)

Following on from what we said yesterday, there are those who argue that because Jesus knew God His Father and was in constant communion with Him, He couldn't have felt loneliness. But that perception fails to recognise that God has made us not only for a relationship with Himself but with others also. It is possible for us to have a good relationship with God, yet at times feel lonely because we have few earthly relationships. And because Jesus took on our human condition, He would have felt the need for human companionship also.

I wonder if, as a child, Jesus must have at times felt apart? He knew that He was in this world not just to be a carpenter but to do His Heavenly Father's business. When His ministry began, it caused dissension in His home town (Mark 6:1–6). Many of those who set out to do the work of God and then meet resistance have someone at home who understands them, but it would appear that Jesus largely lacked that. Some of His family even came to believe that He was deceived (Mark 3:30). On occasions, He would look to His disciples for support, but sometimes in vain. On the eve of the crucifixion they argued about precedence (Luke 22:24). When He was arrested they ran away, and as He was being crucified, with the exception of John, they were nowhere to be seen (John 19:26).

FURTHER STUDY

Isa. 52:13–53:3; Mark 14:43–50, 66–72; Luke 4:28–29, 42–44; 5:12–16

1. In what ways did Jesus experience loneliness in His life?

2. Meditate on Jesus' isolation as He faced death.

Jesus knew the pain of loneliness more than anyone. And, having been in our condition, He can sympathise with us and help save us from that condition. If you are feeling lonely at the moment, then open your heart to Him now. Invite Him to draw near, and without doubt He will.

My Saviour and my God, You who in Your earthly relationships knew loneliness, please draw near to those who carry this kind of pain I pray. Help the lonely to be lonely no more. For Your own dear name's sake. Amen.

An enlarged capacity

FOR READING & MEDITATION – ECCLESIASTES 4:1–12

'If one falls down, his friend can help him up. But pity the man who falls and has no-one to help him up!' (v10)

The question we come to grips with now is this: How does God, the God of all comfort, support us in the pain that comes from loneliness? Well, first we offer it up to Him in prayer so that it can become part of His redemptive plan. Implicit in the offering up of our pain is a willingness to be guided and a readiness to turn our back on any self-pity that may be hiding in our heart.

In my experience, the way God guides the pain that arises from loneliness is to lead the person concerned to a time of gentle self-examination. Circumstances may have brought about a sense of loneliness; equally, loneliness can cause a person to shrink into their shell and unconsciously hold people at bay. Someone has said, 'Anyone can have friendship who will give it.' This may not apply to everyone who is lonely but it may well apply to many. If it is appropriate, be willing to face the challenge.

When we accept that Jesus loves us as we are, and that His challenges are based not on His disappointment with us but on a love that wants to help us develop, then this changes our whole perspective. Ask yourself such questions as these: Is my loneliness partly my own making? Have I sought to develop friendships with others? Do I ask too much of people in return? Have I hindered people's advances by my brusqueness, or even my shyness? Am I willing for Jesus to help me? Do I dwell too much in self-absorption and thus keep others away by downcast expressions? Your openness to these questions will cause Him to draw close to you, not only to deepen His friendship with You but also to help you deepen your friendship with others.

FURTHER STUDY

Psa. 139:1–12; 2 Tim. 4:9–18

1. From what does the psalmist draw comfort?

2. How does the apostle Paul avoid self-pity?

Father, I see that as I seek to enlarge my capacity for friendship I open myself more fully to You. Help me do just this. And help me not to forget to continually thank You for guiding my pain to good ends. Amen.

Praying in God's will

FOR READING & MEDITATION – JOHN 14:1–14

'And I will do whatever you ask in my name, so that the Son may bring glory to the Father.' (v13)

Another pain that arises in the soul of some is the pain of unanswered prayer. My guess is that thousands of you reading these lines are carrying that pain within you and don't know what to do about it. This pain lying unresolved in the soul can sometimes lead to the sabotaging of the Christian life. The spiritual growth of many Christians has come to a halt because they have been unable to resolve the pain of unanswered prayer.

When I was a pastor, I visited a woman one day because I had heard that she didn't plan to come to church anymore. When I enquired if this was true she said, 'Yes, I asked God to help my grandson pass his examination and he failed. God let me down. How can I trust Him for other things when He couldn't help me in a simple thing like that?' My attempts to explain that our prayers are not always answered in the way we wish didn't seem to help her. She was unwilling to face the fact that the child was lacking in natural ability and that perhaps he needed coaching. She blamed the whole situation on God and left the church a bitter and disillusioned woman.

FURTHER STUDY

Psa. 13:1–6; 2 Cor. 12:1–10

1. How does the psalmist resolve the pain in his heart?
2. How does Paul face up to unanswered prayer?

Consider this: prayer would be dangerous if all our requests were answered. I have prayed for certain things over the years that I am glad God did not give me, for I can see with hindsight that if He had then it would not have been good for me. The only prayers that are guaranteed to be answered in the way we desire are the prayers we ask in Jesus' name. In other words, the kind of prayers Jesus would offer were He in our shoes. His prayers were always focused on bringing about the will of God in His life. Let it be so for us also.

Father, if there is pain in my heart over the fact that some of my prayers have not been answered, please help me resolve it once and for all. In Jesus' name I ask it. Amen.

A path through Christian counselling training

Would you like to develop your pastoral care skills? Have you been thinking about training as a counsellor?

Waverley Abbey College equips people to support others in their everyday life and workplaces through biblical care and counselling. From short introductory programmes all the way through to Continuing Professional Development opportunities, the college integrates Christian faith within a Higher Education environment at every stage of learning.

We want to help you explore whether Waverley Abbey College is the right place for you, and so we offer a number of Open Days throughout the academic year. These are a great opportunity to find out more about the different programmes, meet the tutors and hear from current students. We would be delighted to welcome you soon.

For more information about upcoming Open Days, visit **www.waverleyabbeycollege.ac.uk** and book your place today!

MON
20 NOV

An old man's predicament

FOR READING & MEDITATION – LUKE 1:5–25

'Zechariah asked the angel, "How can I be sure of this? I am an old man and my wife is well on in years."' (v18)

The story of Zechariah illustrates, more clearly than almost any other biblical account, the pain that can arise in the heart because of unanswered prayer. Zechariah was serving God as a priest in the Temple in Jerusalem, yet he had a pain deep in his heart. His wife, Elizabeth, had been unable to conceive a child – something Zechariah had prayed about for many years (v13). However, when the angel appeared to tell him that his prayer was to be answered he was unable to receive the astonishing news because, as he put it, 'I am an old man and my wife is well on in years.'

Zechariah had just experienced two amazing spiritual encounters: first, he had been chosen to enter into the Temple and burn incense to the Lord (v9), and second, he had been visited by an angel. Yet despite this he appeared to be quite unable to take in the promise of the angel that his wife would conceive and bear a son. Why, I wonder? Was it because the pain of unanswered prayer was still so acute that it prevented him from reaching out in faith in case he might be disappointed again?

This is only conjecture on my part, but I have seen that situation occur in the lives of many Christians I have counselled. How unexpected it is to observe someone holding back at the very point when they want to move forward. Even though God witnesses clearly to their hearts by His Spirit, they are unable to forge ahead in case matters might not turn out as they expect. May this be a problem for you too? If so, spend a little time in God's presence searching for any disappointment that remains in your heart over the issue of unanswered prayer.

FURTHER STUDY

Psa. 28:1–9; Luke 24:25–35

1. How does the psalmist hold himself steady?

2. Why does Jesus challenge Cleopas and his companion?

Father, hold me steady as I examine my heart. Help me face up to any disappointments over unanswered prayer that may be lingering in my soul. In Christ's name I ask it. Amen.

'Too good to be true'

FOR READING & MEDITATION – LUKE 24:36–49

'they still did not believe it because of joy and amazement' (v41)

Following on from yesterday, when I suggested that Zechariah's seeming reluctance to accept the word of the angel was perhaps due to the disappointment he may have been feeling because of unanswered prayer in the past, permit me to explore with you what may lie behind the strange words in today's reading.

When, following His resurrection, Jesus appeared to the disciples in Jerusalem we are told that 'they still did not believe it because of joy and amazement'. What a strange expression! They 'did not believe because of joy'. Having been disappointed once by reason of the fact that Christ had been crucified, did they now hardly dare to believe in case they were disappointed again? Eugene Peterson, in *The Message*, paraphrases our text for today in this way: 'They still couldn't believe what they were seeing... it seemed too good to be true.' Was the prospect of the pain they would feel if it was not true so great that for a moment they could not give themselves to what they were witnessing? Did they retreat temporarily into the safety of doubt, rather than take the risk of perhaps being disappointed again?

FURTHER STUDY

Gen. 45:25–28; Acts 9:19–30; 11:4–18

1. What convinces the disciples that Saul is genuine?
2. What moves Peter forward into a deeper trust of God?

Again, I can only conjecture. What I do know, however, is that many Christians are locked into situations where, because of unanswered prayers in their lives and the ensuing disappointment, they are afraid to reach out in faith to God, even when, as perhaps today, He might be speaking a direct word to their soul. This is too important an issue to brush aside. He or she who has ears to hear, let them hear what the Spirit is saying to their heart.

Father, help me not to miss one thing You are saying to me. Is this an authentic word spoken direct to my heart? If so, help me receive it and move forward into a deeper trust of You. In Jesus' name. Amen.

'Yes, and always yes'

FOR READING & MEDITATION – ROMANS 11:25–36

'For from him and through him and to him are all things.' (v36)

How can the pain of unanswered prayer become a pain that leads towards life rather than regrets and disappointment? We explore that question now.

Before it is possible to move on past the pain of unanswered prayer in our lives, let's understand and accept that God knows what He is doing, and the way He responds to our prayers is entirely up to Him. The pain will never fully go away until we have acknowledged these two matters. Once we allow the pain in our heart to lead us to a place of openness and we are willing to see things from God's perspective rather than our own, then we will find it is a pain that truly leads to life.

St Francis de Sales, the Catholic preacher and devotional writer who lived in the late sixteenth and early seventeenth centuries, taught his people to greet God's will in all events – even the bitterest – with the words, 'Yes, Father. Yes, and always yes.' And that response, he explains, is not that of stoical endurance but joyfully acknowledging the truth that God always does what is right. Many Christians may grimly boast in the face of difficult situations 'I can take it', but that is not the spirit St Francis taught. He taught that we are to welcome the will of God. Like the apostle Paul, he saw God's will as being 'good, pleasing and perfect' (Rom. 12:2).

Quite simply, learning to trust God's sovereignty in all things resolves the pain of unanswered prayer. And by acceptance I mean joyful acceptance. Learning to accept God's will joyfully, you will find that the pain you have borne leads to life – a new and confident trust in the true and living God. Try it and see.

FURTHER STUDY

Isa. 55:6–13; Luke 22:36–44; Phil. 1:18–26

1. How does Jesus greet God's will in Gethsemane?

2. In what ways does Paul see things from God's perspective?

Yes, Father, I will, but I need Your help. Your ways are beyond my understanding and baffle even the most brilliant minds. Help me not to try to figure everything out, but simply trust. In Jesus' name I pray. Amen.

Heavenly comfort – the best

FOR READING & MEDITATION – PSALM 23:1–6

'Even though I walk through the valley of the shadow of death, I will fear no evil' (v4)

Now we move on to consider a further pain that is felt by the human heart – the pain of bereavement. Can God deal with this pain and provide comfort? With all the conviction of which I am capable, I say He can. Regularly in my writings I return to the issue of grief and loss because always there is someone somewhere who is facing this pain. Perhaps we never need the understanding of how Jesus can help us in our pain more than in that numb hour when we call a loved one by name for the last time and hear only the echo of our own voice.

Bereavement is a difficult pain to face – whether it's sudden or the culmination of a long, tedious journey. There is almost certainly someone reading these lines today who feels caught in the maelstrom of emotions experienced in the early days of losing a loved one. I have often found my words drying up when called upon to minister to people in such an hour as that. Of course, all bereavement is painful, and in some cases the sorrow can be excruciating. C.S. Lewis, when talking about the death of his wife, likened bereavement to having one's leg cut off. The pain eventually stops but one will never be a biped again.

Bereavement, it has been said, is sometimes harder for Christians, especially if the loss is someone young. However, as we hold on to God in the midst of what might be massive confusion and look to Him, we find comfort and consolation. We also thank God for those who offer comfort and company when we experience bereavement. They are to be commended and appreciated for their love and sympathy, but the primary source of comfort in the time of loss is heavenly comfort.

FURTHER STUDY

Isa. 61:1–3; Matt. 5:1–10

1. Why is the Lord's servant anointed with the Spirit?

2. What consolation does Jesus offer?

Lord Jesus, while I am so deeply thankful for all those who support and help in the hour of bereavement, I am even more thankful for the comfort that comes to me from heaven. Thank You dear Lord. Amen.

FRI
24 NOV

'The anatomy of grief'

FOR READING & MEDITATION – 2 SAMUEL 1:17–27

'I grieve for you, Jonathan my brother; you were very dear to me.' (v26)

As someone who has walked with hundreds of bereaved individuals through their hours of grieving and endured many hours of personal pain as the result of the losses in my own life, I have been able in my more lucid moments to piece together what I call 'the anatomy of grief'.

First, there is the sense of shock that brings a numbness to the spirit. Deep down one struggles to come to terms with the fact that death has occurred. One knows it has happened but there is a faint hope that it is all a mistake. Then one feels self-conscious – the result of being awkward in the company of others. What will they think of me if I cry? Should I hold myself together so that others will not regard me as lacking in courage? Often grief is accompanied by a lethargy – the disinclination to make even the slightest effort. And others can unwittingly add to the pain by insensitive remarks such as 'God likes to take the best to Himself' or 'I'm praying for you, so you should be fine.'

Often the worst time for me was in the morning upon waking, when the remembered voice could cause me to retreat like a small afraid child. C.S. Lewis said after the death of his wife, Joy, 'At the very moment when I mourned her least, I remembered her best. It was as if the lifting of sorrow removed a barrier.' I experienced the same thing after losing my own wife.

But, thank God, there is a resolution to grief; it is like coming out of a dark tunnel and seeing the light. Looking back, you realise that God was there as much in the darkness as He is in the light. Hold on, dear bereaved friend. God is supporting you, holding you and is very close by today.

FURTHER STUDY

Jer. 31:10–14; Luke 6:17–23

1. What promises of support are made by the Lord to His people?

2. To what does Jesus promise an end?

Father, help me understand that in the hour of grief I am being upheld, even though I may not be conscious that I am. Thank You for being there for me. In Jesus' name. Amen.

Excessive grief

FOR READING & MEDITATION – JOHN 11:17–44

'Jesus wept.' (v35)

It is not wrong or unspiritual to feel grief. Jesus wept at the grave of a loved one, as we see from our reading today. Some struggle badly with grief; others handle it better. It helps to accept the truth that grief is inevitable and is part of the human condition. We are designed to grieve when a loved one dies. This is something that is not only to be accepted but expected.

There are some Christians who, although they accept grief, can overcome it quite quickly and focus more on their loved one being with the Lord. Sometimes other Christians who are walking with them worry about those who do not appear to be full of grief, perceiving them to be in denial. We are all made differently, and in such situations the bereaved person needs to be given the benefit of the doubt. Their grief is tempered with the knowledge that their loved one is with the Father, and so we should not be too quick to believe that they are avoiding the process of grief.

There are two cautions in relation to grief: one is that a person does not grieve at all, and the other is that they feel excessive grief. In my experience, it took me about nine months to really work through the grieving process. Some come through it much more quickly than that, whereas others take much longer. While appreciating that everyone handles grief differently, we should be aware that excessive grief over a long time may not so much be an expression of love for the person who has been taken away as a sadness for oneself. It may be that for the grieving person there may come a time when, in order to move on, they need, with God's help, to relinquish their hold on the memory of the loved one.

FURTHER STUDY

Job 1:13–22; 3:20–26; Luke 19:41–48

1. In what two ways does Job handle grief?

2. What caused Jesus to feel grief?

Please help me, dear Father, whenever I have to face the pain of grief, to invite You into my loss and not to lose myself in sorrow. Help me to know Your everlasting arms are holding me safe. In Jesus' name I pray. Amen.

SUN
26 NOV

What we receive, we give

FOR READING & MEDITATION – 2 CORINTHIANS 1:1–11

'the God of all comfort... comforts us in all our troubles, so that we can comfort those in any trouble' (vv3–4)

How does God comfort the pain in a heart grieving for loss? Here again, He can do little with it unless we offer it to Him. That a bereaved person finds it difficult to offer to God the pain they are feeling is understandable, but, please believe me, there is great value in doing so. Our Father is glad to be asked for His help.

Often the first thing He does is to assure us that He can sustain a broken heart and a lurching and disoriented mind in the hour when a loved one is taken away, for He Himself, in the Person of His Son, knows what it is to weep at the grave of a close friend – His friend Lazarus. As the comfort of His understanding and sympathy sweeps into the soul, a new courage is given to face the world and we are able to live through the pain with a quiet sense of His presence filling our soul. Reminding ourselves that in a world of pain and sorrow the great God of the universe is not insulated from pain Himself, helps to keep us from cynicism. Again, in the Person of His Son, He said in Mark 14:34, 'My soul is overwhelmed with sorrow to the point of death.' Jesus is, of course, referring to His own death here, but the reality is that the eternal God is not immune to sorrow. He feels, does this great creator.

FURTHER STUDY

Isa. 53:4–11; Rom. 12:9–16

1. How does Isaiah make it clear that God shares our sorrows?

2. How does Paul say Christians should care for one another?

But perhaps the greatest thing God does with the pain of loss is to sensitise our souls to the needs of others. I know I would not have helped others who have been bereaved, had I not walked that way myself. The comfort God gave me as I gave Him my pain is, as today's text assures us, the same comfort I am able to give to others. One day you'll hold hope for others as they have held hope for you.

Father, I know that right now I am not able to fully take in this truth that the comfort You give me I will one day be able to give to others. However, I hold on to it and thank You for that hope. In Christ's name. Amen.

For your church

CWR has been resourcing the Church for 50 years, and today there are a number of exciting programmes for you and your church to discover together. Each includes resources for leaders to explore the teaching on Sundays and at small group meetings, as well as daily devotional books for individuals.

Engage the whole church in pastoral care

Paraclesis: Journeying Together is a six-week series that explores how we all can come alongside and journey with others who are struggling with life's challenges – the way God journeys alongside us.

Know who we are, where we belong and what we are living for

Transformed Life is a seven-week programme based on Ephesians 1–3, which helps us answer three of life's key questions. Gain a strong foundation in knowing who you are in Christ, as well as your true belonging and purpose.

Live out our lives 'in Christ'

Transformed Living is a seven-week programme based on Ephesians 4–6, which explores how we can live life 'in Christ' today through unity, purity and spiritual maturity. (Can be used as a stand-alone programme or together with Transformed Life.)

To find out more, visit **www.cwr.org.uk/foryourchurch**

'I'm so thirsty'

FOR READING & MEDITATION – ISAIAH 55:1–13

'Come, all you who are thirsty, come to the waters' (v1)

The pain we consider now is a pain that is universally felt but not universally acknowledged. I refer to the pain that comes from our unwillingness to let God satisfy our spiritual thirst. This is what I describe as the pain of emptiness. To understand this pain we have to go back to the beginning and consider the way God made us.

When God made us, He built into our beings a longing and a thirst for a relationship with Him. If this is not satisfied, a deep sense of emptiness and pain resides at the core of our being. Almost everyone knows the pain of thirst when we are seriously parched or dehydrated. Diabetics, of whom I am one, experience this more than others. A similar pain occurs in the soul when we are not receiving the life that comes from God; the difference being that water alleviates physical thirst, but there is nothing that can fully satisfy the soul other than the life-giving water that comes to us from God through His Son, Jesus Christ.

Why is it then, you may ask, that many people are not Christians appear to be happy and contented, if there is so much pain in a soul that is bereft of God's resources? Because they quench the deep ache within them by drinking from wells that soothe but do not satisfy. The satisfaction they find is temporary and provides just momentary relief. No one realises what soul satisfaction is until they have drunk of the stream that flows from Jesus. Before I became a Christian, I drank from many different wells but they all left me deeply unsatisfied and somewhat weary. How different things are now. It is Jesus that satisfies and settles my restless spirit.

FURTHER STUDY

Psa. 63:1–11; John 4:7–14

1. How does the psalmist express his thirst for God?

2. What assurances does Jesus give the Samaritan woman?

My Father and my God, how glad I am that I have found in You the satisfaction for my soul's deepest longings. I am so thankful. Amen.

Why Jesus shouted

FOR READING & MEDITATION – JOHN 7:25–44

'Jesus... said in a loud voice, "If anyone is thirsty, let him come to me and drink."' (v37)

As an evangelist who has preached the gospel for many years, I have come to the conclusion that in the main there are two powerful motivations for people coming to Christ. One is the need to be forgiven and the other is the need for fulfilment. These are not the only reasons people turn to God, of course, but they are, I have found, the major ones.

In today's text we are told that on the last day of the feast – the Feast of Tabernacles, held in the autumn when all the crops had been gathered in – Jesus stood in the middle of the people and with a loud voice cried, 'If anyone is thirsty, let him come to me and drink.' Why, I wonder, did Jesus say these words 'in a loud voice'? I think it was because as He looked at the people taken up with the religious ceremonies – all significant and important in themselves – He saw that they were out of touch with the truth that their souls could never find satisfaction in ritualism but only in a personal relationship with Him. This truth, I believe, moved Him so deeply that it caused Him to cry out with a sense of urgency and passion. It was as if He was saying: 'Aren't you aware that deep down inside of you is a thirst that no religious ceremony can quench? Get in touch with it and let it lead you to me, the only one who can truly satisfy the longings of your soul.'

The great tragedy of the ages is that people have lost touch with their spiritual thirst that would lead them to Jesus – the source of all spiritual satisfaction. They would rather drink lukewarm substitutes than come to the pure fresh fountain Jesus provides in and through Himself.

FURTHER STUDY

Isa. 58:9–14; John 6:52–59

1. Where does Isaiah declare spiritual satisfaction can be found?

2. What does Jesus say is real food and real drink?

Lord Jesus, I lift to You today the people in my life who seek satisfaction for their soul's thirst anywhere but in You. Help them, I pray, this very day to understand that You, and You alone, can meet their deepest needs. Amen.

Caught in a cycle

FOR READING & MEDITATION – PHILIPPIANS 3:12–21

'Their destiny is destruction, their god is their stomach, and their glory is in their shame.' (v19)

Over the past couple of days, we have been seeing that when God created us He put within us a thirst for Him. When we turn to sources other than Him for our soul's satisfaction, there arises within us a certain degree of pain, which is really God's way of drawing our attention to the truth that only He can fully satisfy us.

Throughout time, multitudes have kept that pain at bay by attempting to satisfy their spiritual thirst at some place other than God. But, as the story of the woman at the well recorded in John 4 so clearly shows us, over every fountain that this world opens is a sign that reads, 'Whoever drinks of this water will thirst again, but whoever drinks of the water Jesus gives will never thirst.'

In today's text, the apostle Paul speaks of people who 'live as enemies of the cross of Christ', whose god is their appetite or their stomach. It is interesting that the Greek word *koilia* translated 'stomach' is the same word that is used in John 7:38 (the text we looked at yesterday) for the innermost part of us that only Jesus can satisfy. Those who do not know what it means to quench their thirst in God will experience an ache that relentlessly drives them forward to find any relief. An unsatisfied spiritual thirst is acute. It demands relief. After all, who can tolerate pain for too long? And this is how addictions can develop. The relief that comes from taking drugs – or from any other addiction – can temporarily numb the pain. When that happens, people are then caught in an endless cycle of attempting to satisfy their thirst in things, rather than in the true source of life.

FURTHER STUDY

Psa. 16:1–11; Eph. 1:3–14; Rev. 7:9–17

1. List the ways the psalmist's spiritual thirst is quenched.
2. Give thanks for the many spiritual blessings we have in Christ.

Holy Spirit, send revival to our world so that people shall be drawn, not just in thousands but multiplied thousands. In Christ's name I ask it. Amen.

Decision day

FOR READING & MEDITATION – REVELATION 22:12–21

'whoever wishes, let him take the free gift of the water of life.' (v17)

Again let us ask the question: How does God go about guiding the pain we have been considering over the past few days to good and godly ends? He can do so only when the person concerned is aware of the painful thirst that is in their soul, and is willing to stop attempting to alleviate the pain with other remedies and instead drink from the living water that Jesus alone provides.

It may be that somebody reading these words today is in that precise situation. Perhaps over the past few days you have become aware that the restlessness you have in your soul is really a pain that is being numbed by such things as endless activity, food, drink, promiscuity, or denial. Pause with me now and accept the truth that the soul is in pain when it is not in a relationship with God. God wants to use that pain of an unquenched thirst to draw people to Him, as He alone is the thirst quencher and satisfier of the soul's deep longings. Get in touch with what is going on inside you and consider the truth that God has put this pain within you, not to hurt you but to help you find Him.

To paraphrase C.S. Lewis again, pain is God's megaphone to rouse a deaf world. In this case, the pain in your soul is not intended simply to get past your deafness but to draw your attention to the fact that you have a deep unquenched thirst. Find a quiet spot and ask God to forgive your sin, come into your life and fill your heart with His Holy Spirit. Anyone can come. Remember, He's only a prayer away. Turn to Jesus now and drink from His life-giving stream.

FURTHER STUDY

Psa. 107:1–9; Acts 8:26–39; Heb. 11:1–2, 13–16

1. Along with the psalmist, quench your thirst in God's love.

2. How did the Ethiopian discover Jesus for himself?

Lord Jesus, I do so entirely and wholly. I receive You as my Lord and Saviour. Please end the pain in my soul as I look to You for life. In Christ's name I pray. Amen.

The turning triangle

FOR READING & MEDITATION – JOHN 16:1–16

'When he comes, he will convict the world of guilt in regard to sin and righteousness and judgment' (v8)

Now we start to consider another pain that can arise from time to time in the soul – the pain of guilt. Let there be no doubt about this: when sin is present in the soul there will always be pain. Again, God arranged it this way. A little boy in a Christian school who had just listened to a talk on conscience wrote, 'When God created us He put a triangle in our soul that is meant to turn whenever we do wrong – and when it turns, it hurts.' Bill Gothard, an American Bible teacher, defines guilt as 'God's way of drawing our attention to the fact that we have broken one of His principles.'

I once debated with a secular psychiatrist who argued that guilt is something that has been built into us by socialisation – that it is something that has been manufactured over time. I disagreed and said that guilt is not something created by society but something that has been built into us by God. The idea propagated by many is that there is no basis for guilty feelings; that conscience and the moral universe are concepts that must be rejected. But morality is not built up by custom; it is built into the structure of the universe. It exists – before and after any immoral action. Those who commit wrongdoing and think they can escape consequences within a moral universe are sadly mistaken.

FURTHER STUDY

Psa. 38:1–4, 17–22; 1 Pet. 4:1–6

1. When overwhelmed with guilt, what does the psalmist pray?

2. How does Peter contrast Christian and pagan attitudes to sin?

The majority's approach to psychoanalysis is partly to blame for the decline of the sense of guilt in today's world because of the assumption that guilt is a harmful thing. However, although the word 'guilt' may be missing from some modern-day psychology textbooks, it is not missing from the Bible.

Father, I see that You have designed the universe in such a way that I'm most comfortable when I am doing Your will. When I do Your will I experience peace; when I resist it I experience pain. Help me stay in the place of peace. Amen.

False vs real guilt

FOR READING & MEDITATION – 1 JOHN 3:11–24

'This then is how we... set our hearts at rest... whenever our hearts condemn us. For God is greater than our hearts' (vv19–20)

In considering the pain that arises within the soul when guilt is present, it is necessary, I think, to understand that there are two kinds of guilt – false guilt and real guilt. Many suffer unnecessary anxiety and pain through false guilt.

A woman I knew who was a nurse suffered from false guilt because she overslept one day and turned up at the hospital late. She found that a patient of hers had died just minutes before she arrived. The patient, of course, was being cared for by another nurse, who had stayed on after her shift to cover for her. But she blamed herself for the patient's death. Her reasoning was irrational. 'I am sure,' she said, 'that if I had been on time the patient would not have died. God must be very angry with me and will cast me off.' As we talked, it became clear to her that her feelings of guilt were groundless. We also talked around how Jesus did not cast off His disciples who had gone to sleep while He was agonising in Gethsemane. At the close of His time in the garden He said, 'Rise, let us go!' (Matt. 26:46). He then led them on to the next duty. 'Do not dwell on the past,' I advised, 'and move on.' I am glad to say she did. The pain she was feeling was not coming from God but from an oversensitive conscience.

The world is full of people who are guilty of sin and won't allow themselves to feel their guilt but there are many, also, who feel guilty and really have no reason to do so. Let me remind you of the words of today's text: 'This then is how we... set our hearts at rest... whenever our hearts condemn us. For God is greater than our hearts'.

FURTHER STUDY

Psa. 36:1–12; Rom. 8:26–32

1. What marks the difference between the righteous and the wicked?

2. How does Paul help us believe that God is for us?

Father, help me to discern the difference between false guilt and real guilt, between insensitivity and oversensitivity. Make me truly balanced in regard to this matter. In Jesus' name I pray. Amen.

SUN
3 DEC

The tutelage of the Spirit

FOR READING & MEDITATION – ROMANS 9:1–18

'I speak the truth in Christ – I am not lying, my conscience confirms it in the Holy Spirit' (v1)

We are seeing that God has built within us a 'warning bell' that is designed to ring whenever we get off limits and commit sin. This 'warning bell' is our conscience, but here again, as with guilt which can be either real or false, we learn that even conscience in itself can be an unsafe guide. It can both accuse us or excuse us according to the set of beliefs we hold.

A missionary who worked in India tells how when he saw a woman about to throw her baby into the Ganges – the river of India sacred to all Hindus – as an offering to what she believed was the god of the river, he pleaded with her to refrain from such an inhuman act. She reacted by saying, 'But my conscience tells me to do it.' He retorted, 'And my conscience tells me you should not do it.' A conscience not guided by the Word of God is an unsafe guide.

FURTHER STUDY

Eph. 5:15–20; Col. 3:15–17; 1 Tim. 1:3–11

1. How do the Word of Christ and the Spirit feed us?

2. What accompanies a good conscience?

Often we hear people arguing, 'Well, I'm living according to my conscience, isn't that enough?' Sadly no, it isn't enough. Conscience is the capacity to distinguish between right and wrong according to the standards you accept. It can be taught to approve things that are completely contrary to God's declared will. Conscience, therefore, is unsafe unless it is directed by the Holy Spirit and the Word of God. In today's reading, Paul, tells us that his conscience was under the tutelage of the Holy Spirit. What was going on in his conscience was being confirmed by the Holy Spirit. Notice the two safeguards: the truth in Christ (the words that Christ spoke) and the confirmation of the Spirit. Without those two things our consciences can lead us to death rather than life.

Gracious Father, I want my conscience to function in the way it ought – fed by Your Word and the Holy Spirit. Again I pray, please prevent me from being insensitive or oversensitive. Keep me balanced, dear Lord. In Jesus' name. Amen.

The forgiveness of God

FOR READING & MEDITATION – 1 JOHN 1:1–10

'If we confess our sins, he is faithful and just and will forgive us our sins and purify us from all unrighteousness.' (v9)

Again it is time to ask ourselves a question: How does God comfort and guide a conscience that is hurting because of the presence of sin? Feelings of true guilt that are rooted in wrong choices and lifestyles will lead to spiritual restlessness and pain if not guided by God to His solution – forgiveness. The pain of true guilt is inbuilt by God to cause us to seek relief. But where? Not in denying guilt and claiming it is an illusion. Not in suppression or repression or any other kind of psychological talking therapies. Not in saying, 'Let bygones be bygones.' Not in joking about it as Oscar Wilde did when he declared, 'The only way to get rid of temptation is by yielding to it.' No, we are limited on either side by hedges of thorns that press painfully against us if we attempt to stray and take any way other than Christ's. These thorn hedges are the creation of God's mercy; He has provided them so that we should not be comfortable in wrongdoing. Of course, we have to admit our guilt before we can be delivered from it. Deny the problem of guilt and nothing can be done about it. Admit it and at once there is the possibility of a solution.

The first of the 12 steps set out by Alcoholics Anonymous is: 'We admitted we were powerless over alcohol – that our lives had become unmanageable.' The first step in deliverance from guilt is also to admit that we are powerless to do anything about it ourselves and ask God for His forgiveness and strength. Are there any names and places from which you shy away in your memory? Anything for which you need forgiveness? If so, I suggest you take action now. Remember today is the tomorrow you put off yesterday.

FURTHER STUDY

Psa. 130:1–8; Titus 3:3–8

1. On what does the psalmist rely?

2. Of what is Paul sure?

Father God, I turn to You in repentance for any sin there may be in my life. Help me to be led by You all the way if there are issues that need to be dealt with. Your mercy is from everlasting to everlasting. I am so grateful. Amen.

TUES
5 DEC

Childhood woundedness

FOR READING & MEDITATION – MARK 9:33–37

'Whoever welcomes one of these little children in my name welcomes me' (v37)

Some may have difficulty identifying with the next type of pain I would like to consider with you – especially if you experienced love and encouragement in childhood. If this is so, then I would ask you to believe me when I say that the pain felt by those who knew little or nothing of love in their childhood or were subjected to abuse is one of the most distressing of all the pains that can afflict the soul. I call it the pain of childhood woundedness. The degree of pain varies, of course, with the degree of hurt or deprivation. It can be high or it can be low.

In her autobiography, Hillary Clinton writes of how when she was in high school she brought home a straight-A report card and showed it to her father, hoping for a word of commendation. Instead he said, 'Well, you must be attending an easy school.' His thoughtless response may have been no more than a casual quip, but it created a point of pain that continued to persist long after the remark was made.

Hillary Clinton's distress might be regarded by some as a very minor pain, but there are multitudes who still carry a degree of intense pain because of a lack of love or mishandling in their childhood. As I said, it is difficult for those who experienced love and affection when they were growing up to understand how great this pain can be, but it is true to say that for some the pain is as sharp as a thorn in the flesh. A man well into his eighties talked to me about the fact that he never felt loved during his childhood years. Tears ran down his face as he told me his story. Eighty years – and still the pain rankled in his soul.

FURTHER STUDY

Joel 2:28–32; Mark 10:13–16; Acts 2:16–21, 36–39

1. How does Jesus link children with God's kingdom?

2. In what context does Peter reiterate Joel's prophecy, and to what effect?

Lord Jesus Christ, You spoke so clearly about welcoming children in Your name. Help me appreciate more fully the significance of this I pray. For Your dear name's sake. Amen.

A major cause of hurt

WED
6 DEC

FOR READING & MEDITATION – PROVERBS 12:1–18

'Reckless words pierce like a sword, but the tongue of the wise brings healing.' (v18)

We continue reflecting on the fact that many people carry within them the pain of childhood woundedness caused by a lack of love (or perhaps even physical or emotional abuse) on the part of those who raised them. The soul of a person who is not loved is in pain, and that pain, as I said yesterday, can sometimes continue into old age. The man in his eighties to whom I referred yesterday told me that when he was a child his father said to him, 'You will never be any good.' With tears running down his face he continued, 'Here I am more than eighty years later having lived a life in which my father's prophecy has come true. Largely I have never been good at anything.'

As someone who has journeyed with people to overcome their hurts in childhood, I have found that the inner child of the past not only survives into adult life but also thrives. It is so sad that some go to their graves carrying a pain that was implanted in their souls during childhood – a pain that no medication can cure. There is no doubt in my mind that the biggest cause of childhood hurts is ill-spoken words. Physical abuse is terrifying for a child, but so too is the pain the soul feels when it is assaulted by caustic and cutting words.

Today's reading tells us that reckless words pierce like a sword. How true. Negative and harsh words spoken to children in a tone of voice that carries with it resentment and disrespect can live on and affect many adult decisions. Let's be aware of the power of words.

FURTHER STUDY

Col. 3:1–10; James 1:19–27

1. What are signs of being renewed?

2. Which words save and which do not, according to James?

My Father and my God, help me realise the power of words and grant that no words shall pass my lips that will hurt anyone, especially a child. In Jesus' name. Amen.

THURS
7 DEC

Sparks from the tongue?

FOR READING & MEDITATION – JAMES 3:1–12

'Consider what a great forest is set on fire by a small spark.' (v5)

Yesterday we ended with the thought that words have a tremendous, even an awesome, power. Words can bless or they can blister, they can lift or they can load, they can hurt or they can heal, they can bring comfort or consternation. Some comments can make us edgy, especially when spoken in a sarcastic or critical tone of voice. Take this for example: 'You're just like your father.' Or, 'I thought you were taking on more than you could manage.'

The picture James gives us in today's passage is of someone setting a situation on fire simply with sparks from his or her tongue. Speaking for a moment to those of you who are parents, can I ask if you have ever set your child's spirit on fire with resentment and anger or bitterness towards you because of a toxic comment? I once did that with one of my sons and he was well into his teens before it occurred to me to ask him if I had said anything to him during his childhood that was still rankling within him. He broke down and confessed that some words I had said to him in a moment of anger were still burning in his soul. His admission gave me the opportunity of asking for his forgiveness, and at this point the relationship between us changed completely. When later he left home and was married, he would telephone me just to chat for a few minutes. He did that almost every day until he died.

FURTHER STUDY

Prov. 16:12–24; 1 Tim. 4:6–5:2; 6:3–5

1. Study the importance of a disciplined tongue.

2. In what is Timothy to set an example?

Even though we may not be able to erase the unstudied, caustic remarks we have made to our children, we can ask forgiveness for them. It takes a lot to do that, but I know from experience that doing so can transform relationships between parents and children. It really can.

Lord God, once again, I see how an undisciplined tongue can bring so much hurt to people, especially a child. If I have to ask forgiveness of anyone today for ill-spoken words, then help me do so I pray. In Jesus' name. Amen.

Two vital issues

FOR READING & MEDITATION – MATTHEW 6:5–14

'For if you forgive men when they sin against you, your heavenly Father will also forgive you.' (v14)

There are two things I would like to bring to your attention today, the first being the need to follow through on asking forgiveness for any hurt or difficulties you might have caused to someone by your ill-chosen words – especially a child. Children may forget what caused an outburst but they may not forget your response. It is also important to remember that our words will, if they are not forgiven by Jesus, endure beyond death. Jesus said that everyone 'will have to give account on the day of judgment for every careless word they have spoken' (Matt. 12:36).

The second thing I would like to address is the pain that may be in someone's heart right now because of a serious hurt or trauma that happened in childhood. How does God comfort a person with this kind of pain towards life? He will help you first to admit that what happened, happened. Many, I have found, who are in pain from emotional woundedness pretend they are not feeling hurt because they regard it as wrong to criticise those who failed them in their formative years. If you are in pain, face it. You will not get past the pain until you do so. You don't have to indulge it but you must acknowledge it. Once you are at that point God will guide you through the only door that can set you free – forgiveness.

FURTHER STUDY

Psa. 34:11–18; Eph. 4:25–32; Col. 3:12–13; 1 Pet. 3:8–12

1. To whom does the psalmist want us to listen?

2. Why is our forgiveness significant?

Perhaps you are thinking, 'I can forgive many things but not that.' Well, with God's help all things are possible. Hold the painful situation (even many painful situations) in your mind and offer forgiveness to those who caused you such lingering pain. You supply the willingness, God will supply the power. Forgive as you have been forgiven – then let it go.

Gracious and loving Father, the message of forgiveness sounds so wonderful, except when I have to forgive. Help me here, dear Lord. I offer my willingness to You now. In turn, please grant me Your power. For Jesus' sake. Amen.

SAT
9 DEC

Is God good?

FOR READING & MEDITATION – PSALM 119:65–72

'You are good, and what you do is good; teach me your decrees.' (v68)

Once more we move on in order to consider what I am calling the pain of shattered dreams. I am thinking of such things as a business failure, a broken engagement, a marriage that is on the rocks, a career that has hit a roadblock, and so on. In one form or another, many people experience shattered dreams at some point in their lives. Perhaps you are in that situation at this very moment. When that happens the pain can be intense and we look for ways to dull it. In fact many, when they find their dream has been shattered, live just to dull the pain. How sad, when life consists mainly of attempting to deaden the pain resulting from a shattered dream.

A friend of mine has spent time talking to an elderly widow who frequently speaks at meetings and has been a help to hundreds who have listened to her story. This widow had put her experiences in writing, but was unable to find a publisher willing to publish her manuscript. She felt a growing sense of pointlessness, which hurt – and hurt deeply. Of course, there are far more serious shattered dreams than that, but this simply illustrates that when our plans are for some reason crossed or frustrated, pain arises in varying degrees, and the goal then is always to handle the pain.

FURTHER STUDY

Psa. 145:9–21; Mark 10:17–27

1. How does the psalmist link God's goodness with people's pain?

2. How does Jesus link God's goodness with God's will?

But in addition to finding ways to handle pain, a major problem people have to struggle with when dreams are shattered is to maintain hope. Larry Crabb says that the question uppermost in people's minds when a dream is shattered is this: Is God really at work right now? Is He pursuing a good purpose that requires this to happen? Yes, says the psalmist in today's text. I agree. Do you?

Father, I long with all my heart to affirm Your goodness with the same confidence shown by the psalmist. If there are doubts within me, then wash them all away I pray, as I consider this truth over the next few days. In Jesus' name. Amen.

Holding on to hope

SUN
10 DEC

FOR READING & MEDITATION – PSALM 33:1–22

'But the eyes of the LORD are on those who fear him, on those whose hope is in his unfailing love' (v18)

My own experience leads me to believe that maintaining hope is indeed the biggest struggle people have when experiencing the pain of shattered dreams. I have spoken many times before of the famous picture painted by G.F. Watts called 'Hope' but I think it worth repeating. The picture shows a blindfolded woman sitting on a sphere with her head bowed and a lyre in her hand. Only one string of the instrument is unbroken, and in the background of the picture just one star shines in the sky. Two cleaners were seen gazing at it on one occasion and were somewhat mystified by what the artist intended to convey. 'Hope?' said one. 'Why is it called "Hope"?' After gazing for some time at the figure perched precariously on the sphere the other responded, 'Perhaps she hopes she will not fall off.'

Many people think of hope in these terms – as a poor precarious thing. One cynic commented, 'Hope is the most hopeless thing of all.' Schopenhauer, a German philosopher, said, 'Hope is the bait by which nature gets her hook in our nose and makes us serve her interests though they may not be our own.'

However, someone who is familiar with the New Testament knows that hope is not presented like that in its pages. Paul highlights hope as one of the three cardinal virtues of the Christian faith, the other two being love and faith (1 Cor. 13:13). All through the New Testament hope is spoken of in a high and positive way. The writer to the Hebrews uses this daring paradox: 'This hope we have... both sure and steadfast' (Heb. 6:19, NKJV). We would be wise to get hold of this hope before a dream we may have is shattered.

FURTHER STUDY

Psa. 42:1–11; Rom. 5:1–11

1. How does the psalmist hold on to hope?

2. What reasons does Paul give for Christian hope?

Loving heavenly Father, help me to not only understand the value of hope but also what I can hope for when a dream of mine is shattered. Teach me more, dear Lord. In Jesus' name. Amen.

Optimism vs Christian hope

FOR READING & MEDITATION – PSALM 25:1–15

'No-one whose hope is in you will ever be put to shame' (v3)

Often when dreams are shattered and pain fills the soul, one of the first casualties is the loss of hope. We must learn the value of Christian hope, for without it we are at the mercy of the winds of circumstance. I am of the opinion that understanding the importance of Christian hope as opposed to natural hope is one of the most significant lessons we can learn in life.

People who don't know Jesus can rely on a natural hope when things go wrong, but they do not have access to the hope of which the New Testament speaks. One preacher says that the hope which a non-Christian resorts to when faced with shattered dreams is really best described as 'optimism'. We cannot, of course, deny the value of optimism. Someone has commented, 'It may not be full cream but there is something to be said for skimmed milk.' If we had a choice, I am sure we would much prefer to live or work with someone who is an optimist than with someone who is a pessimist. But optimism is a mere shadow of Christian hope. It flourishes where there is little depth of earth and soon withers away because it has no connection with the One in whom all true hope is found – our Lord Jesus Christ.

FURTHER STUDY

Psa. 19:7–14; Titus 1:1–3; Rev. 3:21–22; 4:6–11

1. How trustworthy is the law of the Lord?

2. Of what faith is Paul an apostle?

The hope a Christian has is based on two things: the indestructibility of truth and the fact that God is on His throne. Truth is mighty, and the truth found in God's Word is the mightiest truth of all. It may even be nailed to a cross and taken down as a poor bleeding thing, but it rises again! Then there is the second fact – that God is on His throne. He runs the world the way He thinks fit and allows only what best fits in with His eternal purposes. Never forget that.

Father, help me I pray to hold on to these two truths and let them become as anchors for my soul, not only in times of trouble but in times of triumph also. For Jesus' sake. Amen.

Helping others find **the way home**

The story of the prodigal son in Luke 15 resonates with many people today, especially those grappling with questions of meaning, identity and belonging. Drawing on this parable, and written for those searching for answers, Ron Kallmier introduces his new book *The Way Home*.

'It's likely that we all know someone who has significant questions concerning God and the relevance of Christianity today. Perhaps they have left the Church, or have never set foot in one before. *The Way Home* explores real stories that demonstrate people's different journeys in the search for meaning – and for God Himself. Through the telling of a number of different people's stories, alongside the prodigal son, I hope to encourage readers to think again about their own story, and the deepest issues of faith, life and the nature of God. I believe it will prompt discussion between friends and give opportunities for Christians to graciously walk alongside others who are still searching.'

The Way Home is available from Christian bookshops or direct from CWR. You can use the order form at the back of these notes, or visit **www.cwr.org.uk/store**

ISBN: 978-1-78259-096-5

Plan A vs Plan B

FOR READING & MEDITATION – PHILIPPIANS 2:12–30

'it is God who works in you to will and to act according to his good purpose.' (v13)

How does God guide and comfort the pain that arises in our soul when a dream of ours is shattered? What does He do when He wants to lead us from pain to productivity? We have already (to some degree at least) exposed the secret: He guides us towards hope and enables us to grasp it more firmly. But what do we hope for? That God will restore the shattered dream and bring it to pass after all? Well, He could do that, but not necessarily. No, the hope we have is that God permits only what He can use and that He allows our dreams to be shattered because He sees that His highest purpose for us can be best achieved by so doing. That may be hard to take when we have pinned so much of our own self-worth on the accomplishment of our goals, but as Christians we accept the truth that God does not always work in our way. Behind every shattered dream is a reason known to God.

A friend of mine explains it like this: 'Suppose God said to you, "Here's Plan A and Plan B. You choose. In Plan A most of your dreams will come true. No cancer. No divorce. No heartbreak from your children. But as a result of my satisfying your cherished dreams you will know me a little less. That's Plan A. Plan B is the second choice. I'll shatter some of your cherished dreams in a way that will enable you to glorify me more. You choose."'

Take it from me: behind all shattered dreams in the life of a Christian there is a divine plan. Let the pain lead you to hold more strongly the hope that in allowing your dream to be shattered a greater and wiser purpose has been at work that one day in the future you will acknowledge was the best.

FURTHER STUDY

Gen. 50:15–21; Acts 9:1–6, 11–19

1. How were God's plans fulfilled in Joseph's life?

2. How did God work His purposes out for Saul?

Father, I simply must get hold of this and carry it always in my heart, not just as an opinion but as a conviction. Drive the truth deeper into my soul day by day. In Jesus' name I ask it. Amen.

When unhealthy thoughts persist

WED 13 DEC

FOR READING & MEDITATION – PSALM 55:1–23

'My thoughts trouble me and I am distraught' (v2)

We consider now a further area of pain some people experience – the pain that flares up as a result of wrestling with unhealthy thoughts. Many Christians, I have found, are worn down with the pain and pressure of thoughts that they know they ought not to be thinking but cannot rid themselves of. In some people, all other troubles are minor in comparison with this.

Once I stood in a fairground with a Christian friend. As we stood beside the merry-go-round he pointed out the painted faces of the wooden horses and whispered to me, 'My mind is rather like this merry-go-round – lustful images and wrong thoughts go round in my head all the time. They lash me to such an extent that sometimes I despair and feel I will never be free of them.' Tears fell as he spoke. I saw through those tears deep into his soul and what I saw drew deep compassion from me.

Most of us, I am sure, find wrong thoughts and images arising in our minds on occasions, but think of those who have to fight a battle with them continually. As I have said, there are many in the Christian Church who are engaged in fighting such battles. They are not only assaulted by wrong thoughts but subjugated by them. Because of this, the finer fruits of spiritual growth seldom blossom in their lives. Their sad condition may remain a mystery to those who know nothing of this type of struggle, but God, to whom all hearts are open and all desires known and from whom no secrets are hidden... He knows. And remember, my afflicted or suffering friend, that the divine heart is swift to help those who turn their hearts to Him.

FURTHER STUDY

1 Chron. 28:9–10; Prov. 6:20–29; Matt. 15:10–20

1. What is David's counsel to Solomon?

2. What is it that makes a man unclean, according to Jesus?

God my Father, I am so grateful that there is no problem so great that You cannot deliver me from it. When unhealthy thoughts persist, please provide for me a way of escape I pray. In Jesus' name. Amen.

THURS
14 DEC

A poisoned thought life

FOR READING & MEDITATION – MARK 7:14–21

'from within, out of men's hearts, come evil thoughts, sexual immorality, theft, murder, adultery' (v21)

Some Christian lives are being poisoned from beneath by unhealthy thoughts. Outwardly everything may appear to be fine but there is an underlying problem that will eventually have an effect. They may be compared to some oak trees featured in a newspaper article that needed to be cut down because a gas main beneath them was leaking. The tree surgeon who discovered this said: 'They still looked good but the damage was such that their growth had stopped and it would only be a matter of time before they would appear offensive to the eye.'

You might be surprised to discover how many people in your own church or fellowship who appear to be free of any spiritual struggles would confess to struggling with unhealthy thoughts. If they knew they could confide in someone who would not judge them and be discreet with the information shared, they may, through their confidant's prayer and support, be helped to overcome the problem. Within the confines of the counselling room I have listened to the confessions of ministers, elders, deacons and church officials whose lives seemed to be deeply spiritual, but who were conscious that their spirituality was largely cosmetic because their minds were full of improper thoughts.

The pain such Christians feel as a result of their battle with thoughts they know to be wrong is increased when they realise that they come across to others as being extremely spiritual, and yet they dare not reveal the struggles that are going on within them. One man who suffered in this way – a minister – once told me, 'If people could see into my heart they would spit in my face.' How sad that he should feel so alone.

FURTHER STUDY

Rom. 13:8–14; 2 Pet. 1:1–11

1. How does Paul suggest we combat sinful desires?

2. How may we escape the corruption caused by evil desires?

Gracious and loving heavenly Father, I know Your heart goes out to those whose minds are beset with wrong thoughts. Please help them dear Father. And if this problem occurs in my own mind, help me too I pray. In Jesus' name. Amen.

No indulgence

FOR READING & MEDITATION – EPHESIANS 2:1–10

'All of us also lived among them... gratifying... our sinful nature and following its desires and thoughts.' (v3)

From my own experience of seeking to help those who struggle with improper or unhealthy thoughts, I would say that by far the most troublesome thoughts are those focused on sexual issues. And I have come to believe that these thoughts result from a diseased imagination. I was about to write that the people who suffer from such thoughts are the victims of a diseased imagination, but I checked myself because although in one sense they are victims, in another sense the thoughts persist because they have not learned to take control. It is important to understand that we are not responsible for wrong thoughts arising in our minds, no matter what kind they may be, but as Christians we are responsible for what we do with them after they have arisen. Never indulge a wrong thought. Like the camel's nose in the tent, it will soon occupy the whole space.

This is what I believe happens. A thought comes into our mind, not surprisingly considering our sinful nature and the influence of the corrupt parts of the media. But instead of swiftly out-manoeuvring it, we toy with it and allow it to enter into the citadel of our mind. The struggle with wrong thoughts is usually lost or won in the first moments after they arise because everything turns on how swiftly the wrong thought can be dealt with. If the thought is allowed to remain and the person concerned forgets that every minute it is gathering momentum, the imagination starts to play with it and then it can quickly pass, as someone has put it, 'from inclination to appetite, and from appetite to hunger, and from hunger to craving, and from craving to torment, and from torment to sin'.

FURTHER STUDY

1 Cor. 5:1–11; 10:1–13; 1 John 2:15–17

1. How does Paul deal with sexual immorality?
2. How can we avoid a diseased imagination?

Father, I see that success in overcoming wrong thoughts depends on the speed with which I deal with them. Help me be aware of this and dispatch them, not indulge them. In Jesus' name. Amen.

SAT
16 DEC

Turn your eyes to Jesus

FOR READING & MEDITATION – HEBREWS 12:1–13

'Let us fix our eyes on Jesus, the author and perfecter of our faith' (v2)

Is it really possible to overcome improper or wrong thoughts? Can God take the pain caused by wrong thoughts from the mind and turn the situation around? I answer: yes, He can. How, then, does He do this?

Again I repeat that you must first let the pain lead to the recognition that this struggle cannot be won by human effort alone. The pain must be handed over to Him. Once that is done the strategy Jesus uses is simple but effective: He aims to occupy the mind, and when His presence is welcome and He is enthroned, He will transform every area of life and every tributary of thought. As the writer to the Hebrews tells us, we continually look to Jesus. The struggle with wrong thoughts begins in the mind, and that is where the battle is won or lost. Wrong thoughts are not driven out by sheer willpower – even when this is done prayerfully.

To give these thoughts sustained attention, even if the intention is to ask God to forgive them, can be unhelpful because the more they are considered, the deeper they burn themselves into the mind. They are to be dealt with by swiftly directing the mind to a purer and more absorbing theme. And there is no purer and more absorbing theme than Jesus. Hence the wisdom of knowing Jesus as a personal friend and turning the mind at once towards Him. He is the centre of all things pure. To think of Him is to summon His aid. The thought that seemed so seductive a moment before looks repugnant when we are conscious of Jesus' presence. So don't wrestle with wrong thoughts. They will pin you to the mat every time. The remedy is not to fight but to fix your eyes on Jesus. I know of nothing better.

FURTHER STUDY

2 Cor. 10:1–6; Phil. 4:4–9; 2 Pet. 3:1–2; 1 John 3:1–7

1. What is wholesome thinking?

2. What incentive does John give for purifying ourselves?

Lord Jesus Christ, how can I ever thank You enough for the truths that flow from Your Word? Help me grasp the fact that success in overcoming wrong lies not in tussling but in turning – turning my eyes on You. Amen.

A strong picture of Jesus

SUN
17 DEC

FOR READING & MEDITATION – PSALM 141:1–10

'But my eyes are fixed on you, O Sovereign LORD; in you I take refuge' (v8)

I feel drawn to spending another day reflecting on how improper or wrong thoughts can be overcome. So far, I have focused mainly on lustful thoughts because in my experience they are by far the most common of the mind's troubles. But the same course of action applies to other wrong thoughts too – jealous thoughts, for example, or vengeful thoughts. The secret is always to turn the mind swiftly to Jesus. Thousands of people who have struggled with wrong thoughts testify to the success of this simple principle – myself included.

To some all this might sound too simplistic, so let me urge anyone struggling with wrong thoughts to develop within himself or herself a strong picture of Jesus. This can be done by meditating on the picture of Jesus presented in the Gospels and praying that the Holy Spirit will make Him clearer to one's mind and dearer to one's heart. If Jesus does not become a living reality and the person concerned does not develop a keen ear for the words of Jesus and direct their lives accordingly, when they try to turn to Him in the moment of overwhelming temptation, they will not have as clear a picture as they ought of the transforming Christ. The art of navigation is best learned before you find yourself in a storm. Those who do not prepare in advance to deal with issues that may arise should not be surprised when they find themselves unable to cope.

I can only hope and pray that if the pain of wrong thoughts fills your mind, it will cause you to stop trying to overcome them in your own strength and start resting not just your eyes but also your faith on Jesus.

FURTHER STUDY

John 3:16–21, 31–36; Heb. 7:20–28; Col. 1:15–20

1. What picture does John give us of the transforming Christ?

2. What view of Jesus should we cultivate?

Saviour, increase my understanding of Scripture so that my knowledge of You equips me for any crisis that may occur in my life. For Your name's sake I pray. Amen.

MON
18 DEC

The problem of physical pain

FOR READING & MEDITATION – GENESIS 3:1–19

'God did say, "You must not eat fruit from the tree... and you must not touch it, or you will die."' (v3)

Our thoughts up to now have been on mental and emotional pain, but it would not be appropriate to end these meditations without saying something, as I promised, about physical pain. All of us will have experienced physical pain at some stage of our lives; some have to live with it on a permanent basis. Today's passage shows that as a result of Adam and Eve's sin, God warned that pain would enter their lives. Presumably, had they not sinned, childbirth would have been pain-free, the ground would not have been cursed, and Adam and his descendants would not have had to struggle to maintain their existence.

There is no crystal-clear answer as to why physical pain is part of God's universe. The best explanation (in my view) is that God, knowing Adam and Eve would fall, built into them the warning system of pain. This meant that they would be alerted when things went wrong with their bodies and, because of sin, they started to deteriorate. As we said earlier, if there had been no pain, the human race might not have survived. It has been argued that a loving God should have given us a switch that we could use to turn off pain, but common sense tells us that had He done so, most people would turn off the switch permanently.

Ultimately, we have to leave this matter with God and recognise that though we are big enough to ask questions we are not always big enough to understand the answers. We may not like it, but it is the answer that Christians must settle for. Indeed, many of the questions that arise in our hearts in this life will have to wait for answers in eternity.

FURTHER STUDY

Prov. 3:5–8; Isa. 40:12–14, 21–31; Luke 5:17–26

1. What sort of God ought we to trust, according to Isaiah?

2. Why did Jesus surprise the Pharisees and amaze the crowd?

Father God, once again I see that everything comes down to trust. Thank You for reminding me that though I'm big enough to ask questions, I may not be big enough to understand the answers. I believe – please help my unbelief. Amen.

The God of all comfort

TUES
19 DEC

FOR READING & MEDITATION – PSALM 103:1–22

'As a father has compassion on his children, so the LORD has compassion on those who fear him' (v13)

We continue reflecting on the matter of physical pain. You will not be surprised, I am sure, when I tell you that research shows the main reason why people refuse to acknowledge God or lose their faith in Him is because they cannot find an adequate answer to the question of how a good God can allow pain in His universe.

C.S. Lewis said that if anyone had asked him when he was an atheist, 'Why do you not believe in God?' he would have replied that with so much pain in the universe he found it impossible to believe that creation is the work of a benevolent and omnipotent Spirit. The thing that Lewis did not consider as an atheist (and which he came to see later) was that despite the existence of so much pain, myriads of human beings in the past millenniums have attributed creation to a wise and good creator. The more he thought about that, the more he realised that unless we know God and have confidence in His Word, the Bible, there is just no way we can reconcile a loving and omnipotent God with the issue of suffering.

Ultimately, as I said yesterday, it all comes back to believing a loving God has a purpose in allowing pain that more than compensates for the suffering and sorrow we experience when our bodies feel pain. The thing that we who are Christians must hold on to is that although we cannot fully understand all the issues surrounding physical pain, at least we have the promise of God's comforting presence in the midst of our pain. Some may regard that truth as a psychological ploy that we use to console ourselves. Millions know it, however, as reality.

FURTHER STUDY

Job 42:1–12; Isa. 40:1–2; 1 Thess. 4:13–18; 5:9–11

1. How does Job deal with the issue of suffering?
2. With what words does Paul offer comfort to the Thessalonians?

Father, I am so grateful that when I am in pain, in addition to the painkillers that medicine provides, because of my relationship with You I have access to another source of comfort. Thank You dear Father. Amen.

Just saying His name...

FOR READING & MEDITATION – HEBREWS 13:15–21

'Through Jesus, therefore, let us continually offer to God a sacrifice of praise' (v15)

Yesterday we said that the problem of physical pain has caused more people to deny the existence of a God of love than any other thing. Sir Arthur Conan Doyle, who was a doctor as well as a writer of detective stories, tells in his autobiography that what made him an agnostic in early life was something he could not reconcile with a merciful providence. This is his account of the incident: 'I was called by a poor woman to see her daughter. As I entered the humble sitting room there was a small cot at one side, and by the gesture of the mother I understood the sufferer was there. I stooped over the little bed expecting to see a child. What I really saw was a pair of sullen brown eyes full of pain. I could not tell how old the creature was. Long limbs were twisted and coiled, the face was sane but malignant. "It's a girl," sobbed the mother. "She's nineteen. Oh, if only God would take her."'

FURTHER STUDY

Mark 10:46–52; 1 John 5:1–12

1. What did Bartimaeus call out?

2. Who is it that overcomes, according to John?

When encountering a terrible situation such as that, it is not easy to maintain faith in a loving God, so please let me share with you my personal experience here. At the time of writing these notes I have been in quite considerable pain with the cancer that has afflicted my body. At times it has been almost unbearable, but painkillers have helped. Thank God for painkillers. These I regard as part of the providence of God. Of course, God can and still does heal, and I hold on to that truth in the face of everything. But I have found also that when in the midst of pain, crying out to God in prayer is a relief too. I can't adequately explain it, but somehow, when in pain, just speaking out the name 'Jesus' seems to bring Him incredibly close.

Lord Jesus, what power there is in Your lovely name. Let it be a remedy for all Your children who struggle with physical pain anywhere and everywhere in the world today. Amen.

A childlike trust

FOR READING & MEDITATION – PSALM 56:1–13

'When I am afraid, I will trust in you.' (v3)

The task of a minister or other person who has the care of souls is not easy when one has to sit with someone who is in intense pain. The question, 'If God loves me, why does He let me suffer like this?' is a difficult one to deal with, and I know some ministers who have left the ministry because they did not have a clear answer to this question.

Longstanding readers of *Every Day with Jesus* may be familiar with my reflections and referencing of the best-selling book written by Rabbi Kushner entitled *When Bad Things Happen to Good People*. Rabbi Kushner struggled to reconcile the goodness of God with the illness of his son, who died at the age of 19 from progeria – an ageing disease that made his teenage son like an old man of 90. The Rabbi's verdict was that God is good, but because sin has tampered with His universe He can no longer gain control over evils such as physical disease. His conclusion was that God's love is still certain but that His power is limited.

The book became a bestseller because people saw the Rabbi's conclusion as an acceptable solution to the problem of why a good God allows bad things to happen in His universe. But it is not a true answer. God's power is not limited by sin. The Bible makes it absolutely clear that He is as much in control of the universe now as He ever was. Take this, for example: 'The LORD is the everlasting God... He will not grow tired or weary, and his understanding no-one can fathom' (Isa. 40:28). As Christians, let's be careful not to compromise our beliefs by accepting half-answers that make us feel a little less confused but in the end undermine our ability to trust.

FURTHER STUDY

Isa. 26:1–13; Rom. 3:21–26; 6:8–14

1. How does Isaiah encourage trust in God?
2. How does Paul say God deals with sin?

Father, please drive this truth deeper into my soul for I see so much depends upon it: I must trust You even when I cannot trace You. Give me a childlike trust I pray. In Jesus' name I ask it. Amen.

Turned to good effect

FOR READING & MEDITATION – HEBREWS 2:1–13

'it was fitting that God... should make the author of their salvation perfect through suffering.' (v10)

The issue facing us now is this: we've explored how God can guide our emotional pain to good and godly ends but can He do the same with physical pain also? Yes, when we offer it up to Him He not only comforts us with His presence but deepens our sensitivity to the pains of others.

Today's text reminds us that Jesus was made perfect through suffering. I think that this principle may also apply to us though in a different way. Jesus was made perfect in that He became the perfect Saviour who opens up the way to God. Although Jesus' experience of suffering was unique, I can say I am all the better for the suffering in my life. There is something about suffering that puts steel in the soul when God is invited into it. That is not to say that I am brave in the presence of pain. C.S. Lewis once wrote, 'You would like to know how I behave when I am experiencing pain, not writing books about it. You need not guess, for I will tell you; I am a great coward.' That is my testimony too. I may not be brave but I am better for the pain. Now I pray with much more concern for those who suffer and my prayer life has taken on a depth that I never thought possible.

FURTHER STUDY

Isa. 38:1–6, 9–20; 1 Pet. 1:3–9

1. How does Hezekiah's suffering turn to good effect?

2. How can Christians rejoice in times of suffering?

I find comfort, too, in knowing that when I pray I am coming to One who has felt physical pain, perhaps as few have ever felt it. Our dear Saviour knows what it is to be in agonising pain. The fact that He too has suffered helps more than words can convey. From the bottom of my heart I say it: I would rather be in a world of pain and have the knowledge of God than be in a world where there is no pain but without the knowledge of Him.

Father, suffering may not be palatable but it is persuasive – especially when I see how pain and suffering deepens our sensitivity to the needs of others. Thank You that You can guide even physical pain to good and godly ends. Amen.

Next Issue

JAN/FEB 2018

Pursuing God

Have you ever wondered why some people seem to have a more vibrant and intimate relationship with God than others?

Writing from his experience in pastoral ministry and counselling, and with his characteristically sensitive approach, Selwyn helps us consider the things that can come between us and our heavenly Father – and how we can overcome them with God's help. Most of all we learn that the pursuit of God is not about a set of rules, but an amazing grace-filled adventure.

Also available as eBook/ eSubscription

From the Jan/Feb issue, single issues will be £3.25.

See order form for updated subscription prices.

Obtain your copy from CWR, a Christian bookshop or National Distributor.
If you would like to take out a subscription, see the order form at the back of these notes.

SAT
23 DEC

'Christmas pain'

FOR READING & MEDITATION – LUKE 2:21–35

'And a sword will pierce your own soul too.' (v35)

In the few days that lead up to the celebration of Christ's birthday we shall focus on something that some refer to as 'Christmas pain'. Studies show that more people become depressed at Christmas than at any other time of the year. It is also the period when rates of self-harm rise to their highest level.

In today's reading, we come across the startling words which Simeon spoke to Mary: 'And a sword will pierce your own soul too.' I wonder what Mary thought of that disturbing remark. One moment she was experiencing the thrill of holding the incarnate Son of God in her arms, and the next moment she was being told that as a result of His coming into the world a sword would pierce her soul. Simeon's prediction, I believe, had reference to the sufferings that Jesus would have to endure later in life, and of which Mary, His mother, would be a witness.

Strangely, the prediction made by Simeon to Mary seems to apply to millions of people the world over during the period in which we celebrate Jesus' birth, though the form of suffering is completely different. This season seems to bring a sword that pierces many a soul. Christmas may bring joy and cheerfulness to some but to others it brings great pain. The theatres may be full and the shops and streets festooned with lights but for many this just accentuates the pain they are feeling in their hearts. Let's be sensitive at this special time of the year to those who carry some inward pain and not expect them to put on a happy face just because it's Christmas. The pressure to come up to expectations is often what pushes such people over the edge.

FURTHER STUDY

Neh. 8:1–12; Psa. 30:1–12

1. Meditate on Nehemiah's words to the grieving people.

2. How does the psalmist react to his own mixed feelings?

Father God, please help me to be conscious of the needs of others. May I be aware of the pain that some are carrying at this season of the year. Give me a heart that is sensitive and perceptive. In Jesus' name. Amen.

'Be happy, it's Christmas'

SUN
24 DEC

FOR READING & MEDITATION – PHILIPPIANS 2:2–11

'Each of you should look not only to your own interests, but also to the interests of others.' (v4)

As we have noted, more people fall into depression at Christmas than at any other time of the year. Why? The main reason is that during this season the expectation, as we said yesterday, is almost always, 'Be happy, it's Christmastime. Drop all expressions of sadness and put on a happy face.' It is rather like the situation some children find themselves in when they are taken for the first time by their parents to the seaside and are told, 'Now we have brought you here to enjoy yourself, and enjoy yourself you must.' People who may not feel like joining in the festivities at Christmas because of some inner sadness they are experiencing, find the pain increasing when they are put under pressure and urged to enjoy themselves. When this causes them to feel resentful, they try to repress the feeling, and repressed resentment is one of the factors that contributes to depression.

There is another factor to consider too. Some years ago a psychologist devised a stress test, which he used to demonstrate that the period of Christmas itself carries with it a significant amount of stress. Buying the right presents, sending out the cards, organising events for the children – all these things increase the stress factor, he said. Most of us could have told him that without the help of a test!

What does all this say to us as Christians? It says that we ought to take notice of the text at the top of this page and ask God to help us at this season of the year to consider not simply our own needs, but the needs of those for whom Christmas may bring added pain.

FURTHER STUDY

Rom. 14:5–21; 15:1–6

1. How does Paul define the kingdom of God?

2. How does Paul counsel us to be sensitive to others?

Father, again I ask You to give me a heart that senses the sorrows of others. And help me not to be a pressure but to relieve the pressure. In Jesus' name. Amen.

MON
25 DEC

If Christ had not come

FOR READING & MEDITATION – 1 TIMOTHY 3:1–16

'He appeared in a body, was vindicated by the Spirit, was seen by angels, was preached among the nations' (v16)

On this Christmas Day I think it appropriate, bearing in mind our theme, to reflect on the fact that the world into which our Saviour came is a world of deep pain. Those who see only lovely sunsets, beautiful scenery and mother-love are not looking at the whole world. I often think of Oswald Chambers' comment, that 'Life is more tragic than orderly.' There will be some reading these lines today whose hearts are heavy with grief and whose world has been turned upside down. If we are honest, there are times when it seems less like God's world and more like the devil's world, and there are some who believe that God has been excluded from His own world by the concerted efforts of the devil and sinful men and women. But it only seems that way. It is His world still.

Please understand this is part of the message of Christmas: the Son of God entered this world of pain and suffering, wore our flesh, measured its frailty, and grew and struggled with the same problems with which we struggle. Before He died for us on the cross and was raised from the dead for our justification, He left this message with His followers: 'be of good cheer, I have overcome the world' (John 16:33, NKJV).

So, in all the growing madness of things, in the frustrations and bitterness of the hour, come and pause by the manger and hear and know the truth of good news: this child will feel the bitterest of pains, but this will enable Him to enter into our sorrows and pain and understand us. He is able to enter into our condition because He has been in our condition. Always remember: you were dear enough to God for the Saviour to be born.

FURTHER STUDY

John 1:10–18; Gal. 4:4–7; 1 John 4:9–16

1. Into what sort of world did Jesus come?

2. Why did Jesus come?

My Father and my God, help me focus on the fact, once again this Christmas Day, that had Your Son not come to this world I would still be lost. His coming into this world has changed my life forever. Amen.

'God's red flag'

FOR READING & MEDITATION – 2 TIMOTHY 1:1–12

'Christ Jesus... has destroyed death and has brought life and immortality to light through the gospel.' (v10)

As we are now drawing to the close of our meditations on the God of all comfort, for the rest of our time together I would like to emphasise some of the main truths we can hold on to as we move into the future. Think of these truths as anchors for the soul. Some of them have been raised in our meditations; some will be new.

The first is the reminder that in a fallen universe pain has a positive function. It is God's red flag run up to warn us of hidden danger. Pain stabs us awake and says, 'Look out, there is something wrong here. Attend to it.' Although we are not able to fully comprehend why God allowed pain to enter His world, we can certainly understand that pain has a positive purpose and why, as we said earlier, it has been called 'God's preventative grace'.

The Christian faith survived the worst that could ever happen to it – the physically and spiritually painful death of its founder. No one has ever experienced such deep darkness and awful pain as the Son of God endured on calvary. But by His life and death He has filled the earth with new hope. And now Christianity proclaims the message that the worst thing that ever happened – the crucifixion of the Saviour – has become the best thing that happened – the redemption of human beings and the joy, if they accept that salvation, of spending eternity with Him. A faith like that has survival value and will outlast all the shallow-rooted and hollow philosophies of life. Nothing else enables us to stand up to the troubles and trials of life. Christianity is unique and invincible. No other faith has such a message, no other faith has such a Saviour.

FURTHER STUDY

2 Tim. 2:8–13; Heb. 11:32–40; Rev. 1:4–8

1. What kind of faith has survival value?

2. What testimony does John give to Jesus Christ?

Lord Jesus Christ, help me remember when life is difficult that I belong to a Saviour who has not only made life possible, but full of possibilities. I am so thankful. Amen.

Know God, know life

FOR READING & MEDITATION – EPHESIANS 1:15–23

'I keep asking that... God... may give you the Spirit of wisdom and revelation, so that you may know him better.' (v17)

A second matter relating to pain that I would like to bring before you in these last few days is this: when we experience pain, let's always be willing to admit that we are doing so. Sadly, when some Christians feel pain they pretend that they don't. They base their refusal to acknowledge their pain on Jesus' instruction, 'Do not let your hearts be troubled' (John 14:27) and reason thus: if we admit to our pain we are going against the words of Jesus, so we will pretend we are not feeling it. What did Jesus mean when He said, 'Do not let your hearts be troubled'? Was He really telling us that we ought not to feel pain? Are we to go about pretending that we are not in pain when in reality we are?

Larry Crabb says, 'We Christians are often practising Buddhists because we kill desire to avoid pain then wonder why we don't enjoy God.' You may be aware that according to tradition, one day in India's history Siddhartha Gautama was meditating under a tree when he came to believe that the way to end pain and suffering is to end desire. He later referred to himself as the Buddha (the awakened one) and taught what he called the 'four noble truths'. 1. Life is suffering. 2. The cause of all suffering is desire. 3. The way to end suffering is to end desire. 4. Spend your life learning to eliminate desire. This, however, is not what Jesus teaches.

Jesus teaches us that the way to handle pain is to discover your built-in desire for God and deepen it by longing to know Him in all His fullness. When you do this, you will see that everything that happens in your life, both good and bad, becomes redemptive and moves you towards the God you desire.

FURTHER STUDY

John 10:9–10; Col. 1:9–14; Heb. 11:1–6

1. What quality of life does Jesus promise?

2. What does God give us in Christ?

Gracious and loving Father, I have asked before that You will make me a person of integrity – and I do so once again. Help me to see that nothing can be changed until it is first admitted. In Jesus' name I ask it. Amen.

Don't waste your pains

THURS
28 DEC

FOR READING & MEDITATION – JEREMIAH 51:58–64

'the peoples exhaust themselves for nothing' (v58)

A further thought to remember as we seek to build into our minds some of the key issues we have been considering over the past weeks is that unless pain is working to some end it breaks us by its meaninglessness. James Moffatt translates today's text in this way: 'Pagans waste their pains.' The point the prophet Jeremiah is making in this verse is that those who live without a God-reference – the 'pagans' – don't know what to do with their pains and thus waste them. Their pain ends in mere dull, fruitless and meaningless suffering. It gets them nowhere. One of the biggest problems psychologists have to deal with is the problem of meaninglessness. Christians have the advantage – God gives meaning to everything.

So much of the world's pain is being wasted, as politicians and other leaders try to deal with issues on their own, and do not bow to the wisdom of God that is to be found in Scripture or ask for His help in prayer. They apply their worldly remedies that are frequently opposed to the principles of Scripture and find after a while that they are back where they started and compelled to go through the whole miserable business all over again.

We can learn to make our pains productive by bringing them to God and asking for His help in making them redemptive. Only when we see redemption in pain can we have any release from it. Purposeless pain is paralysing. 'Pain can be taken up into the purposes of God,' said Dr E. Stanley Jones, 'and transformed into finer character, greater tenderness and more general usefulness.' As in childbirth, so pain, when used by God, can bring forth new life.

FURTHER STUDY

Psa. 119:25–32; 2 Cor. 4:7–18

1. How does the psalmist turn his pain over to God?

2. How did Paul make his pain productive?

My Father and my God, help me not to waste my pains but to always turn them over to You for You to do what You so wonderfully do – to turn the worst into the best. Amen.

FRI
29 DEC
'The secret centre of the soul'

FOR READING & MEDITATION – PSALM 10:1–18

'You hear, O LORD, the desire of the afflicted; you encourage them, and you listen to their cry' (v17)

Yet another thing to keep in mind concerning pain is that there are depths in our soul that sometimes only pain enables God to reach. Let me explain.

One of the great saints of the sixteenth century was a Carmelite mystic and poet known as St John of the Cross. Towards the end of his life he was imprisoned in a tiny cell built into the wall of the prison in Toledo, Spain, by those who opposed his reform of the Carmelites. During the nine months of painful imprisonment, he became conscious that there were depths within him that he had not yet opened up to God. The pain led him to cry out, 'Why have You hidden, Beloved, and left me groaning? You fled like a stag having wounded me. I went in search of You and You were gone.' Later, out of the pain of his longing for God there went up such a cry that it brought a revelation from Jesus which thrilled his soul and led to him writing *The Living Flame of Love,* in which he describes Christ's love in these words, 'Flame, alive, compelling, yet tender past all telling, reaching the secret centre of my soul.'

FURTHER STUDY

Psa. 46:1–11;
1 Tim. 1:12–17

1. From whom is the Lord a refuge?
2. What gave Paul cause for praise?

Sometimes it takes pain in our soul to discover that there are parts of us that God has not yet reached. I know from my own experience that in the hours when I have cried out in pain, God has entered into those spaces in my soul from which hitherto He was locked out. That is why, when I look back and see how God has used the soreness that I have sometimes felt in my soul, I am able now to say, 'Blessed pain.' Enduring pain is hard going but the benefits far outweigh the cost! Is there pain in your soul at this moment? Let it lead you to cry out to God until His flame reaches also to 'the secret centre' of your soul.

Lord Jesus Christ, my cry goes up to You. Let that living flame of love that reached into the secret centre of St John of the Cross reach also into my inmost being I pray. In Jesus' name. Amen.

Hand it over!

SAT
30 DEC

FOR READING & MEDITATION – ROMANS 8:1–17

'those who live in accordance with the Spirit have their minds set on what the Spirit desires.' (v5)

As a further reflection on pain, I would add this: the experience of pain always causes us to make a choice. The choice is whether we will try to handle it ourselves or turn it over to God. So often when we are confronted with some difficulty in life our fallen sinful natures try to persuade us that we can handle it on our own without having to bring it to God. The sooner we come to the conclusion that life is not all about us, the better we will be. God wants His purposes to be worked out in our souls, but so often we are deaf to His advances.

As I have just said, attempting to handle things on our own is the way of our fallen nature. In order to stop walking according to the sinful nature and start walking in the Spirit of God, we learn to listen to what our pain is telling us and let Him lead us along the path to life. What I find so sad about the lives of many Christians is that within them lie great pools of pain, which they never think of offering up to God so that He can guide the pain to some redemptive purpose. The verse, 'Ask and it will be given to you' (Matt. 7:7) is probably the most overlooked text in the Word of God.

Please permit a personal question: What pain might you be holding onto that you have been unwilling to hand over to God? Don't keep your pain to yourself and experience purposeless suffering, when God can use the pain to turn you to Himself and give you a spiritual revelation that will result in you becoming a better person and enable you to walk along the road that leads to life.

FURTHER STUDY

Psa. 61:1–8; 62:1–8; Gal. 5:16–26

1. What does the psalmist encourage us to do?

2. How does Paul describe life in the Spirit?

Father, Your Word goes like an arrow to the roots of my problem. Forgive me that for so long I have held on to my pain. I release it into Your hands now for You to turn it into something redemptive. Thank You, Father. Amen.

SUN
31 DEC

Thank God – no more pain!

FOR READING & MEDITATION – REVELATION 21:1–7

'He will wipe every tear from their eyes. There will be no more death or mourning or crying or pain' (v4)

Since we have spent two months together considering the theme 'The God of all comfort', you might be beginning to realise that it isn't always healthy to feel good! Sometimes the soul has a difficult time opening up to what God wants to achieve within it unless it is arrested by pain. When we see what pain when guided by God can accomplish, then we will forever thank Him for it. At the threshold of another year, we cannot guarantee that there will be no more pain because we live in an uncertain and fallen world. But we can be confident that our God can not only lead us through the pain but we can know Him as the God of all comfort in it.

Our last thought, however, must be this: one day we will live for ever in a pain-free world. In today's reading, John lists what will be missing in heaven, and in the text chosen for today he tells us that among other things 'there will be no more... pain'. God's great handkerchief of love will be taken out and will wipe every tear from our eyes – and never again will pain be present in our souls. The reason for this, of course, is that all the causes of pain will be removed – death, disappointment, rejection, loneliness, emotional deprivation, and so on. No funeral cortege will ever snake along the heavenly hills. We will have a joyful and pain-free existence in the presence of our Saviour for all eternity. What a wondrous prospect! Many a person has told me that in the midst of their pain and suffering they have found great comfort in this fact.

I don't know about you but as I contemplate it, I find my heart crying out with all the intensity and passion that is within me:

FURTHER STUDY

Isa. 35:8–10; 1 Cor. 15:50–58; James 1:12; 2 Pet. 3:8–13

1. What transformation will finally take place?

2. What do we have to look forward to?

'O day of rest and triumph, delay not your dawning. Let the angels be sent forth soon to gather the elect. Let the promises be fulfilled which bear in their train all the matchless glories.' Even so, come Lord Jesus. Amen.

Order form

EDWJ N/D 2017

4 Easy Ways To Order

1. Phone in your credit card order: **01252 784700** (Mon–Fri, 9.30am – 5pm)
2. Visit our online store at **www.cwr.org.uk/store**
3. Send this form together with your payment to: **CWR, Waverley Abbey House, Waverley Lane, Farnham, Surrey GU9 8EP**
4. Visit a Christian bookshop

For a list of our National Distributors, who supply countries outside the UK, visit **www.cwr.org.uk/distributors**

Your Details (required for orders and donations)

Full Name:	**CWR ID No.** (if known):
Home Address:	
	Postcode:
Telephone No. (for queries):	**Email:**

Publications

TITLE	QTY	PRICE	TOTAL
Total Publications			
UK P&P: up to £24.99 = **£2.99**; £25.00 and over = **FREE**			
Elsewhere P&P: up to £10 = **£4.95**; £10.01 – £50 = **£6.95**; £50.01 – £99.99 = **£10**; £100 and over = **£30**			
Total Publications and P&P (please allow 14 days for delivery)		**A**	

All CWR adult Bible reading notes are also available in **eBook** and **email subscription** format. Visit **www.cwr.org.uk** for further information.

Subscriptions* (non direct debit)

Subscriptions* (non direct debit)	QTY	PRICE (including P&P) UK	Europe	Elsewhere	TOTAL
Every Day with Jesus (1yr, 6 issues)		£16.95	£20.95	Please contact nearest National Distributor or CWR direct	
Large Print *Every Day with Jesus* (1yr, 6 issues)		£16.95	£20.95		
Inspiring Women Every Day (1yr, 6 issues)		£16.95	£20.95		
Life Every Day (Jeff Lucas) (1yr, 6 issues)		£16.95	£20.95		
Mettle: 15–18s (1yr, 3 issues)		£14.75	£17.60		
YP's: 11–14s (1yr, 6 issues)		£16.95	£20.95		
Topz: 7–11s (1yr, 6 issues)		£16.95	£20.95		
Total Subscriptions (subscription prices already include postage and packing)				**B**	

Please circle which issue you would like your subscription to commence from:

JAN/FEB MAR/APR MAY/JUN JUL/AUG SEP/OCT NOV/DEC *Mettle* **JAN–APR MAY–AUG SEP–DEC**

*Only use this section for subscriptions paid for by credit/debit card or cheque. For Direct Debit subscriptions see overleaf.

We would like to keep you up to date about all aspects of CWR, its ministry and offers. Please tick here to receive information by email ☐ by post ☐

Continued overleaf >>

<< See previous page for start of order form

Payment Details

☐ I enclose a cheque/PO made payable to CWR for the amount of: **£** ______

☐ Please charge my credit/debit card.

Cardholder's Name (in BLOCK CAPITALS) ______

Card No. ☐☐☐☐ ☐☐☐☐ ☐☐☐☐ ☐☐☐☐

Expires End ☐☐ ☐☐

Security Code ☐☐☐

Gift to CWR

☐ Please send me an acknowledgement of my gift **C** ______

Gift Aid (your home address required, see overleaf)

giftaid it

I am a UK taxpayer and want CWR to reclaim the tax on all my donations for the four years prior to this year **and on** all donations I make from the date of this Gift Aid declaration until further notice.*

Taxpayer's Full Name (in BLOCK CAPITALS) ______

Signature ______ **Date** ______

*I am a UK taxpayer and understand that if I pay less Income Tax and/or Capital Gains Tax than the amount of Gift Aid claimed on all my donations in that year it is my responsibility to pay any difference.

GRAND TOTAL (Total of A, B & C) ______

Subscriptions by Direct Debit (UK bank account holders only)

One-year subscriptions cost £16.95 (except *Mettle*: £14.75) and include UK delivery. Please tick relevant boxes and fill in the form below

☐ *Every Day with Jesus* (1yr, 6 issues)
☐ Large Print *Every Day with Jesus* (1yr, 6 issues)
☐ *Inspiring Women Every Day* (1yr, 6 issues)
☐ *Life Every Day* (Jeff Lucas) (1yr, 6 issues)

☐ *Mettle*: 15–18s (1yr, 3 issues)
☐ *YP's*: 11–14s (1yr, 6 issues)
☐ *Topz*: 7–11s (1yr, 6 issues)

Issue to commence from

☐ Jan/Feb ☐ Jul/Aug *Mettle* ☐ Jan–Apr
☐ Mar/Apr ☐ Sep/Oct ☐ May–Aug
☐ May/Jun ☐ Nov/Dec ☐ Sep–Dec

CWR **Instruction to your Bank or Building Society to pay by Direct Debit**

DIREC Debi

Please fill in the form and send to: CWR, Waverley Abbey House, Waverley Lane, Farnham, Surrey GU9 8EP

Name and full postal address of your Bank or Building Society

To: The Manager ______ Bank/Building Society

Address ______

Postcode ______

Originator's Identification Number

4	2	0	4	8	7

Reference ______

Name(s) of Account Holder(s) ______

Branch Sort Code ☐☐☐☐☐☐

Bank/Building Society Account Number ☐☐☐☐☐☐☐☐

Instruction to your Bank or Building Society

Please pay CWR Direct Debits from the account detailed in this Inst subject to the safeguards assured by the Direct Debit Guarantee. I understand that this Instruction may remain with CWR and, if so, d will be passed electronically to my Bank/Building Society.

Signature(s) ______

Date ______

Banks and Building Societies may not accept Direct Debit Instructions for some types of account